CONTENTS

Ships in Focus Publications

Correspondence and editorial:
Roy Fenton
18 Durrington Avenue
London SW20 8NT
020 8879 3527
rfenton@rfenton.demon.co.uk

Orders and photographic:
John & Marion Clarkson
18 Franklands, Longton
Preston PR4 5PD
01772 612855
shipsinfocus@btinternet.com

Printed by Amadeus Press Ltd.,
Cleckheaton, Yorkshire.
Designed by Hugh Smallwood, John Clarkson and
Roy Fenton.

SHIPS IN FOCUS RECORD
ISBN 978-1-801703-96-3

SUBSCRIPTION RATES FOR RECORD

Readers can start their subscription with any issue,
and are welcome to backdate it to receive previous
issues.

	3 issues	4 issues
UK	£24	£31
Europe (airmail)	£26	£34
Rest of the world (surface mail)	£26	£34
Rest of the world (airmail)	£31	£41

C000055632

Our fiftieth issue is a milestone at which celebrate. The editors would like to take the opportunity back on a half century of issues in an extended editorial, whilst also including a couple of features in this issue which reflect their particular interests and backgrounds.

Most important, however, is to thank our readers and contributors for supporting 'Record'. Their features, photographs, feedback and – above all – enthusiasm have made it possible for us to keep going. More on this anon.

We have to admit that the decision to launch 'Record' was taken somewhat casually. When John suggested it to Roy early in our career as publishers, he uncovered a long-standing ambition to edit a journal. We also ought to confess that our projection as to our likely circulation was several times higher than what was eventually achieved. A significant reason for this has been that we could not contemplate the waste and expense involved in putting 'Record' on to news stands, entering a market where vast quantities of unsold printed material is routinely pulped.

If we were disappointed by this shortfall in take up, then we have been more than compensated by the loyalty and enthusiasm of our readers. Editing a journal, even one with the limited outreach of this one, has been every bit as fulfilling as we expected. It is not an opportunity, Murdoch press-like, to inflict one's opinions on the public, but to welcome, absorb and incorporate the input and good sense of contributors, readers and reviewers. As is said of teaching, an editor learns a great deal from those he addresses.

Our choice of a title has not, it seems, been as memorable as we hoped. It was intended to indicate that the journal would indeed be a record, as accurate as authors and editors could make it, and which would also publish corrections and additions to previous features. It also allowed us to title our correspondence column 'Putting the Record straight'. However, it is clearly forgettable, because many readers persist in referring to it as 'Ships in Focus'!

Living up to our ideals over accuracy has created much work and indeed heartache for the editors. We have learnt which contributors strive to get it completely right and which benefit from a little gentle checking of their work (something we willingly do). Beyond this we have striven, and often failed, to eliminate typographical errors. However, compensation has come from the assiduity with which readers have embraced our desire for correctness and have rarely failed to tell us when we have fallen short of our aspirations.

What of the future? We find ourselves facing a demographic trend in which shipping enthusiasts are getting older and not being replaced by younger models. We also hear predictions about the forthcoming demise of print media as it succumbs to its electronic counterpart. Perhaps because we belong to a pre-electronic generation, the editors are not persuaded by the latter concern, and do not believe that a computer screen offers the best way to appreciate a blend of text and photographs. We also believe that interest in any kind of history – not just shipping history – might wax and wane but is unlikely to die completely. No-one alive remembers the American Civil War yet alone the last English one, yet interest in both is strong, to the extent that enthusiasts re-enact these conflicts. It is a moot point as to which will finish 'Record': the prophesied decline in readers or a desire to surrender editorial chairs for rocking chairs. Needless to say, we intend to give readers ample notice if either looks likely!

John Clarkson

Roy Fenton

RARE STANDARD TRAMP SHIP PHOTOGRAPHS

John Lingwood

For most of the twentieth century, commercial ship photography around the North East coast of Britain, was mainly carried out by one or other of two South Shields based firms, W. Parry and Sons Ltd. and Frank and Sons, and few new buildings from the shipyards of the rivers Tyne, Wear, Blyth and Tees escaped their lens whilst carrying out endurance and speed trials over the Hartley and, after the Second World War, Newbiggin, measured miles laid out north of the Tyne.

As a result, both of these companies were able to compile an immense photographic record of merchant and naval vessels built locally. However, during the Second World War ships could not be photographed at sea because danger from German air attacks and mine laying operations meant that trials were not carried out. Nevertheless, some shipbuilders did attempt to maintain their own photographic records, and this article is built around work undertaken on behalf of Bartram and Sons of Sunderland, mainly by Parry, which has produced an interesting portfolio illustrating some of the tramp ship designs initiated by the British Government, and built between 1939 and 1946.

The war, of course, came hard on the heels of the Depression years of the 1930s when many shipbuilders went out of business, whilst others, unable to win orders, simply closed their gates and laid-off their work force, retaining only a skeleton drawing office staff kept busy developing what was to become a new era of so called 'Economy Ships'. Using the expertise of improved model tank testing facilities at the National Physical Laboratory at Teddington and elsewhere, and also benefiting from the more efficient marine engines being tested, a number of new designs were produced and, helped by the Government's 'Scrap and Build' and Shipping Loan programmes, orders began to flow again into British yards in the middle of the decade. Bartram's new standard design was particularly successful, resulting in eleven cargo ships of about 9,000 deadweight being included in the Sunderland shipyards' collective total of 24 ships delivered between 1936 and 1939.

No doubt this design would be amongst those assessed, as war clouds began to gather towards the end of the decade, by the relevant British government departments charged with looking for prototypes of the most-needed classes of vessel which might be required, if war was declared and which, by utilising the new prefabrication methods being introduced about this time, could be built quickly by as many shipyards as possible. History tells us that it was another Sunderland design, produced by J.L. Thompson, which was selected in this exercise as the basis for what was to become an extensive range of British and Canadian built 9,000/10,500dwt cargo ships, and eventually for the US 'Liberty Ship'. The progressions of British-built versions of the Thompson design introduced during the war were identified as 'PF (partially fabricated) with a suffix, beginning with the (X) and (Y) types, and followed by PF(A) to PF(D). In line with Government policy, most of these ships carried names prefixed *Empire*.

Despite this pre-planning many shipyards could not immediately adopt these new standard designs due to lack of berth capacity and inadequate facilities, whilst others were committed to work in progress on contracts signed before hostilities commenced. For all these reasons Bartram's first launch of the war (on the 27th November 1939) was a vessel, *Harpagus*, whose design was derived from those developed during the 'Scrap and Build' period. Built for J. and C. Harrison of London, she was completed in April 1940 and was followed into service on the 24th June 1940 by sister ship *Harpalyce*, shown in the accompanying photograph taken by Parry when lying at the Numbers 1 and 2 conveyor belts of Sunderland's South Dock coal staithes. She would almost certainly be taking on coal bunkers prior to making her maiden voyage. Sadly on the return leg of this, *Harpalyce* was torpedoed north west of the Orkney Islands only two months later. It will be noted that at this early stage in the war, little or no defensive armament had been fitted, other than provision of an A-frame for streaming minesweeping paravanes over the bow.

Five months later Parry reversed his vantage point to set up his camera on the west side of the South Dock, near to the conveyors, to photograph another Bartram pre-war contract, *Richmond Hill*, the second of two sister ships ordered by Counties Ship Management, the recently-formed British flag subsidiary of the Greek Rethymnis/Kulukundis/Mavroleon group. The antiquated, manually operated, derrick arrangement which had provided basic cranage in the yard for decades, and the bows of a ship under construction on one of the building berths, can be seen behind *Richmond Hill*, which is nearing completion at the River Wear

Commissioner's East Quay. Not evident in the photograph is the distinctive shape of the midship section which was a feature of the Isherwood 'Arcform' design to which these two vessels were built.

Richmond Hill completed the back log of Bartram's pre-war contracts, allowing them, at last, to build ships to the account of the Government's Ministry of Shipping (later Ministry of War Transport). However, the lack of facilities at the South Dock shipyard, highlighted by the dated lifting arrangements noted above, meant that these were not to any of the standard, partly-prefabricated designs which formed

the backbone of the Government's emergency programme. Instead, the yard was permitted to construct ten vessels of its own design which featured a flush deck, and had two cargo holds forward, and two aft of a midships superstructure split by a Number 3 hold and a cross bunker. Like the later Ministry designs, the ships were completed with a 'closed shelter deck' which allowed loading to a deeper draught with consequent greater deadweight, necessary to load the heavier military cargoes now being carried.

To photograph *Empire Deed*, the last ship of this group, as she lay at the coal conveyors, Parry returned to the East Quay, and the ensuing print clearly shows how the standard of defensive armament had increased in the two years since *Richmond Hill* was completed. Notable also are the long derricks stepped port and starboard from the fore and main masts, from which anti-torpedo nets could be suspended (it would be interesting to know how effective these were), whilst the row of port holes in the 'tween deck abreast the main mast, show the position of the temporary accommodation provided for the personnel of the Royal Maritime Artillery who manned the DEMS (Defensive Equipment Merchant

Ships) armament, which now included guns mounted at each end of the midships deckhouse. In line with the requirement to load heavier cargoes, derrick capacity has been increased with heavy lift booms at numbers 2 and 4 hatches.

To illustrate what *Empire Deed* might have looked like had she been photographed on sea trials, a print doctored by Parry to delete all vestige of dockside installation is shown. Note that a bow wave has even been added to provide realism: sixty years later what fun Parry might have had using today's computer facilities!

Thanks to an extensive modernisation programme including re-aligned slipways served by Butters Monotower travelling cranes, the Bartram yard was finally able to undertake construction of Ministry standard designs during 1943. The PF(A) design had never left the drawing board and was quickly superseded by the PF(B) type, which featured a long midship structure, split to include Number 3, and a small Number 4 hold, the latter doubling as a cross bunker. *Empire Tourist*, completed in October, was the second of five contracts for vessels of this type allocated to the yard. In Parry's original photograph the stern of a tug towing her out of the South Docks can just be seen, however, the most significant feature is probably the enhanced armament including a forecastle mounted gun. Alas, this was given little time to protect *Empire Tourist* which succumbed to a torpedo in the Barents Sea whilst sailing in the RA57 homeward bound convoy from Russia just five months after completion: recorded as the only vessel lost from that convoy.

By mid-1944, the South Dock shipyard was building to the latest PF(C) design. Although of similar dimensions to the PF(B) type, these vessels differed by having a composite midship superstructure with three holds forward and two aft, and a very small Number 4 hold abreast the funnel.

The PF(C) type also featured a sunken, or 'half height' poop, barely visible above the upper deck bulwark, whilst the derrick complement now included both 30-ton and 50-ton lifts to assist cargo handling at Murmansk. Noticeably, the paravane 'A' frame and the torpedo net derricks seem

to have been dispensed with, but a second gun position has been located aft. However, when Parry photographed *Empire Aden* at Numbers 1 and 2 staithes in May 1945, the forward gun had not yet been fitted.

Bartram's first PF(C) type vessel, although launched as the cargo-ship *Empire Penang* on the 10th July 1944, never sailed under that name, having been completed for the Admiralty as a maintenance ship for hull repairs, equipped with a whole range of workshop machinery for use during what was expected to be a long drawn out conflict with the Japanese in the Far East. For this purpose she was renamed *Mullion Cove* with the pennant number F 186.

Including this vessel, five PF(C)s were completed at the South Dock, and to all intents and purposes they were the last units of the Government's wartime standard tramp ship programme delivered into ownership of the MOWT by Bartram, although further government contracts had been received. These were for ships of yet another design modification, designated PF(D), which differed from the PF(C) only by virtue of a full-height poop. Both these designs sported V-shaped, flat, transom sterns, heralding a form of construction which was to become virtually a standard feature of most cargo ship designs to this day.

Only two PF(D) type vessels were completed by Bartrams, hull numbers 305 and 306, and neither was destined to sail under MOWT ownership. Although the Government Emergency Programmes had been implemented with a view to maintaining control of building, owning and operation of all ships built during the War, private owners had always been allowed to build ships under licence to their own account, providing they conformed to laid-down wartime design standards. With the war in Europe now approaching its conclusion, conditions were eased and, as a consequence, hull number 305 was sold prior to building commencing to British India Steam Navigation and was launched in August 1945 as *Pemba*.

In 1944 BI had received permission to acquire six MOWT contracts to rebuild their depleted fleet and, although little modification was allowed to the standard designs, DEMS accommodation on some of these vessels, including *Pemba*, was converted to provide somewhat spartan cabins for 12 passengers.

Bartram's second PF(D) type vessel, 306, did start life under MOWT ownership and was launched on 16th December 1945 as *Empire Southwold*, but was sold whilst fitting out to Houston Line and completed as *Hesperia*. It is interesting to note that the shipyard called on 'the other South Shields photographer' Frank and Sons to record these two vessels, with the print of *Pemba* apparently 'at sea' showing off their ability to also doctor photographs. The original view of the ship was taken as she lay at the Sheers Quay in the South Dock, with the sheer legs which had been used to outfit countless Wear built ships over many decades visible over the stern of the vessel, and almost overshadowing one of the ultra-modern Monotower cranes, recently installed in the Bartram yard.

Amongst Bartram's output of ships built to MOWT account were three vessels built in accordance with the Government's licensing scheme mentioned above. Reardon Smith took delivery of *Jersey City* in 1942 and *Indian City* two years later. The former was built to the yard's own standard design and was, therefore, a sister of *Empire Deed*, whilst *Indian City* was a PF(B) type, photographed by Parry whilst fitting out at the East Quay, against a backdrop of the North

Eastern Marine engine works. The third licensed vessel was another PF(B) type *Stanrealm*, completed in 1944 for the Stanhope Steamship Co. Ltd.

London owner Kaye, Son and Co. Ltd had also obtained a licence to place an order for a vessel which would have been completed as one of the Government's standards. However, the changing war situation allowed them instead to build to a design developed in-house by Bartram which, although never repeated, clearly exhibited some of the features which were to make the yard's post war tramps so attractive. It was Frank who set up a camera on the deck of a tug to take this sea-trials photograph of *Margay*, the last of the 26 tramp ships delivered by Bartram from their Second World War programme.

With the conflict in Europe coming to an end the Government quickly shifted its shipping priorities to the continuing conflict in the Far East. The 9,000/10,000 deadweight tramp ship was no longer a priority: instead a series of ship designs more appropriate to requirements in that area was introduced and empty berths all over the country were soon filled with orders for coastal vessels suitable for operations in that region, Bartram's allocation being two dry cargo, and two tanker, coasters. As far as Parry and Frank were concerned, they continued in business for a decade or so before being edged out of ship photography by competition from aerial photographers using skills developed during the war.

ROBERT COCK, APPLEDORE SHIPBUILDER
Michael Guegan and Roy Fenton

Appledore has a special place in British maritime history. Not only was it one of the final strongholds of coastal sail, it was also the site of one of Britain's very last merchant shipbuilding yards. This article focuses on shipbuilder and repairer Robert Cock and Sons, the first to build in iron and steel at Appledore, and also completes 'Record's' survey of steam coaster builders in north Devon.

The year 1753 was the earliest date found for a ship built at Appledore by Grahame Farr, who lists a number of local sites for wooden shipbuilding: Irsha Street, Sea Gate, the Pill, New Quay and Hubbastone. Farr names William Yeo as the builder who converted the Pill at Appledore into the Richmond Dry Dock in the 1850s. Yeo took the dock's name, not from the towns in Yorkshire or Surrey, but from Richmond in Prince Edward Island where his father James had an extensive ship building business. James Yeo's ships were sailed across the Atlantic and dry docked at Appledore for completion and survey prior to sale. Contemporaneously, a Thomas P. Cook began building at New Quay in 1852.

The Cock family at Appledore
The first member of the Cock family that can be traced to Appledore was a William Cock, born at George Nympton near South Molton, Devon in 1804, although it is his older brother James in whom we will be most interested. James was born in 1800, also at George Nympton, and seems to have followed William to Appledore in the 1820s.

William Cock learnt his trade as a maltster, and it was as such that he came to Appledore to run the Tavern, situated at the bottom of Meeting Street. Today the Tavern has become the Seagate Hotel, and its relationship to the river as it was at that time was important to the beginnings of the business. When William came to Appledore the Tavern was situated close to the water's edge, the tides lapping the shore not very far from the front door. The 1841 census lists both William and James as living in Appledore.

Bideford shipping registers show that William Cock, innkeeper, became part owner of the sloop *Instow* of Bideford on 27th August 1831 when he purchased 24 of its 64 shares. Another part owner was John Beara, a member of an old established Appledore family. William Cock and John Beara had a loose partnership over several decades, owning several ships between them.

James Cock appears in the 1841 census as a carpenter, and that for 1851 lists him as a master carpenter employing four men, two probably being his sons who were also carpenters. The term carpenter covers many sins and it is possible that they were already repairing ships. James Cocks had four sons all of whom were born at Appledore, his eldest, another James, drowned off St Ives, Cornwall aged 20 on 26th December 1849 when the brig *Chepstow* of Bideford, part owned by his father, foundered with all hands in a storm. James' second son, William, died in 1853, aged 24, probably from cholera. The third son Roger probably

worked at the Tavern Yard with his father as also did the last and youngest son, Robert. Roger died in February 1856, the cause of death being given as 'drowned himself while being lunatic and distracted'. He was just 24 years old.

The Cocks' first ship yard dates from about 1853: a brief family history published in the 'Bideford Gazette' in June 1903 claiming that son William founded the venture and, on his death, his father took over. The Tavern was still being managed by William Cock, James senior's younger brother, and the yard was situated on the land beside the Tavern. It seems that the Tavern Yard, as it became known, was a completely new venture and did not take over any existing site, with the yard's single launch way being tight against the wall of the Tavern. Incidentally, the site has never been built over, and now serves as the Seagate Hotel's car park.

When James the elder died in 1866, Robert was left in sole charge, aged 29 and the only survivor of the four sons. His father had completed six registered vessels plus a pilot boat for Swansea. Most of the work at the yard was ship repairing, short term work and for ready money: new building tied up too much capital for far too long and was never the mainstay of the yard's work. Until 1881 Robert continued the same pattern of work as his father before him, mainly repairs with a small number of new builds. He completed just six registered vessels plus another pilot boat, but the 1870s were hard times for builders of wooden ships. Demand declined rapidly and this decade saw most wooden ship builders in Devon go out of business.

Of the established North Devon firms only Robert Cock survived apparently unscathed; Cox, Johnson, Waters, Clibbett and Cook all went under. Westacotts at Barnstaple almost failed in 1878 when the owner of a new schooner refused to take delivery, but overcame this crisis and carried on until 1884 as shipbuilders, but the glory days had long gone. William Pickard, who had launched his first vessel in 1863 at the Richmond Yard, survived the lean 1870s mainly through ship repair work, but gave up the lease of the Richmond Yard in 1881, the year he launched his last ship. At least he retired leaving a viable business; when he died nearly 20 years later he left a considerable amount of money.

Iron and steel
Robert Cock had realised that wooden ship building and repair was almost dead and on Christmas Day 1881 he took the lease on Richmond Yard and Dry Dock with the expressed purpose of repairing iron and steel ships. Indeed, until 1906 nearly all the vessels repaired at the Richmond Yard were iron or steel sailing vessels. By 1885 the repair business had become so successful that it was causing concern among the Swansea ship repairers because of the amount of work it was obtaining from that port; so much so that the ship repairers held a meeting with the major ship owners about the problem. The owners claimed that, because of a shipping slump, cost was more important than ever. They submitted comparative

figures showing that keeping a ship in Richmond Dock cost £1 per day, whilst keeping one in a Swansea dock cost £10 per week. The cost of a shipwright at Appledore was 4s per day whilst at Swansea it was 6s per day. Repairing ships at Appledore offered a saving of about one third of the cost.

In 1891, after John Westacott went bankrupt whilst working at New Quay, Robert Cock took over the empty site plus all the stock including the moulds for the schooner that John Westacott had recently completed, and worked that yard also. It was here that he built all his schooners of the 1890s. Up until his death, eight of his new builds had been initially registered in his own name. He sold them on as soon as he could find a buyer. In 1902, after a break of five years, Robert Cock and Sons recommenced wooden shipbuilding, this time at the Richmond Yard, all vessels being launched from the same single slip. None were owned by the builders.

In 1906 the Cardiff-registered iron steamer *James Speir* (535/1890) became the first powered craft to be repaired in the Richmond Dry Dock; she was the victim of a collision that left a large gash down her port side. From now on most of the work was on powered craft and in 1908 a member of the family began taking photos of the ships coming in to be repaired. This quite comprehensive record of photos has survived and when comparing with the various comings and goings from the yard as given in the 'Bideford Gazette' it means that dates to within a week can be placed on most of the photos.

On 8th February 1898 Robert Cock died suddenly from influenza, aged 61. He never lived to see the effect of the changes instituted just before the end of his life. Only a month after his death it was announced that the company had won an order to build 12 72-foot steel barges for a London brickworks.

Whether Robert and his sons simultaneously worked all the yards that he had occupied is open to doubt. The Tavern Yard was in business from about 1853; in 1882 Cock took over Richmond Yard and Dry Dock and in 1891 the Newquay Dry Dock and launch way. In total these covered enough ground, and had sufficient dry docks and launch ways, to cover any demands made on the company. However, Robert and his sons then took over yet another site, that of William Clibbett's old yard at the end of New Quay Street; this later became known as the Iron Yard. This yard was then equipped with some new and some secondhand machinery bought from 'a northern yard', beginning the first steps towards the Cocks becoming builders of steel ships. Great play was made of the fact that

Robert's two sons, partners in the firm since 1896 when its name became Robert Cock and Sons, were trained naval architects. In reality, the wooden vessels that Frank Cock and James Cocks designed were almost identical to the vessels the family had built over the previous 40 years.

The first new build was launched on 6th July 1898. A photo shows the name *Primus,* but whether it was her official name is not known, as most of these barges were never registered. The 'Bideford Gazette' gives brief details of the first barge to be launched in its 12th July 1898 issue, but gives no name. The issue for 22nd November reports that the *Lancer* and the *Sirdar,* built for H. Harcourt of Kent, left in tow for Greenwich during the week previous and that the wooden barges *Kathleen* and the *Enid* also left the port under tow for the Woking, Aldershot and Basingstoke Canal Company. The first real ships to be built of steel were the three-masted schooner *Doris* and the steamer *Torridge,* both of 1904. Wooden shipbuilding concluded in 1906.

Until 1920 there were no cranes in North Devon that could lift the engine or boilers into a ship, so some were towed to Bristol and then towed back for completion or else were towed to another port and finished there. Apart from numerous barges only four almost identical steel schooners, one coaster, three tugs and two drifters were completed before the First World War. Also steam powered were the *Ludham Castle* and the *Boy Billy,* both completed in 1904, but these had wooden hulls. Repair of iron or steel ships, both sail and steam, was concentrated at the Richmond site with most wooden craft being taken to Newquay for repair. In 1906 P.K. Harris took over Newquay and soon proved himself a serious competitor when it came to repairing small wood schooners and ketches. P.K. Harris also ran the Hubbastone Yard, sited hard against Newquay, just up the river. Four years before, in 1902, Frank and James Cock began an even more ambitious expansion, that of a completely new building yard further up river from the Newquay/Hubbastone site. It was reported in January 1903 that a new footpath and retaining wall had been built and that foundations had been laid down for various sheds and stores. In July 1905 the 'Bideford Gazette' noted that the new docks were being taken in hand with a view to speedy completion, and that Sir John Aird, who had built Barry Docks, had secured the contract. Although nothing much else about this project was mentioned again, it is interesting because, 70 years later, Appledore Shipbuilders completed their yard at Bidna using part of the 1903 to 1905 wall as their seaward boundary.

In September 1906 the business was converted into a limited company, Robert Cock and Sons Ltd., with a capital of £30,000 divided into £5 shares. Besides Frank Cock and James Cocks (who had decided to alter his name from Cock), there were five other subscribers.

Non-standard coaster hulls

The failure of British Government shipbuilding programmes to make good the severe war losses amongst coasters led to a vast inflation of the price of these craft. As a result a number of shipyards were either set up to build these hulls or – like the Cocks – expanded their horizons to embrace coaster construction. Those

A steel barge described as *Primus* about to be launched on 6th July 1898. *[Michael Guegan collection]*

The Richmond Dry Dock was used for repair work and fitting out vessels built by the Cocks. The steamer *Cloch* (745/1883) of George Bazeley and Sons Ltd., Penzance and the Brixham trawler *Cariad* were under repair during August 1908. *[Cock Collection/North Devon Museum Trust]*

Pulteney (358/1899) in the dry dock in May 1915 when she was owned by John Williams of Scorrier. *[Cock Collection/ North Devon Museum Trust]*

Orchis in Richmond Dry Dock: fitting out during April 1917 before being painted grey (above) and in the 1920s (below). *[Both: Cock Collection/North Devon Museum Trust]*

laid down at Appledore are described in Farr's monograph as standard hulls which were part of the Government's belated coaster-building programme. There is considerable doubt about this, however. Firstly, although all were 150 feet long, the hulls were not to the size built by any of the other yards building coasters for Government account. Secondly, a 'War' name has been found only for the third, yard number 185, delivered in December 1919. And thirdly, the first hull completed, *Orchis*, was delivered to the builders themselves in February 1918, at a time when any ship ordered by the Government would have been registered in the name of the Shipping Controller. It seems likely that the Shipping Controller stepped in to either order or perhaps take over the second hull (completed in February 1919 as *Ortona*) and certainly did so for the third hull which was at one time intended to be *War Wharfe*. In the event, however, all were registered at completion in the name of Robert Cock and Sons Ltd., including the fourth hull, completed as *Orenie* to the same dimensions exactly three years after *War Wharfe* had been delivered as *Orleigh*. It seems very likely that laying down the original yard number 183 was a private venture by the Cocks, who foresaw the likely shortage of coasters.

Steam coaster design had not altered much since at least 1890, and small constructional details have to be examined to differentiate between those from various yards. It has to be said that the Cocks' coasters were not particularly inspired examples of design, at least aesthetically. Sheer was largely confined to the extremities of the hull, and the two masts were rather stumpy, with this and the omission of a mizzen no doubt being economy measures. The open, match-boarded bridge was typical of the time, wheelhouses generally being fitted to steam coasters only in the 1930s or even later. Superstructure was painted in the rather dismal stone colour, whilst funnels were yellow with a black top. *Orchis* was photographed several times with a black funnel bearing the letters WL indicating a charter to Walford Lines of London.

Above: Naval ratings, to man her gun, on board the *Orchis* at Appledore, 27th July 1918. *[Cock Collection/North Devon Museum Trust]*
Below: *Orchis*, still in wartime grey, loads a coal cargo. *[Mrs. J. Smale]*

Below: *Orleigh* is launched on 28th June 1919. *[Cock Collection/North Devon Museum Trust]*

Cock received few orders in the 1920s, and Farr records just seven barges being completed between 1923 and 1931. Alongside running the four coasters, James Cocks also took on management work for local owners. The ship involved, *Ualan*, was one of a number of steamers built in the Netherlands towards the end of the First World War with a view to finding a British buyer anxious to profit from the coastal boom. By 1922 she had passed to George Rossiter of Topsham and William A. Holman of London, who put her in Cocks' hands. Management continued until 1927, by when she had been named *Orpen* (suspiciously like other Cocks' coasters), when she left the British register for another phase of her remarkably varied career.

The Cocks' bold decision to operate the four coasters themselves was undoubtedly a mistake, given their lack of experience and the generally dismal freight rates

prevailing in the 1920s once the post-war boom had passed. Judging by other owners' experiences, the four coasters would have barely met their running expenses, never mind paying off their construction costs. Harris, whose family were Cocks' biggest rivals, speaks highly of them, and claims they tried very hard to stay in business and 'went down fighting'. In March 1932 it was resolved to liquidate the business, and in May of that year the four coasters left Cocks' ownership. At least two were sold by creditors. *Orenie* is listed in the company's closing accounts as being mortgaged, and her mortgagees arranged her sale. According to the customs register for *Orleigh*, she was also repossessed and disposed of by her mortgagees.

There was a fifth coaster hull begun by Cock. Work ceased on this, yard number 187, when it was almost ready for launching. The story goes that the captain-owner of a passing coaster noticed the incomplete hull and arranged to buy it. P.K. Harris and Sons, who took over the yard after Cocks' failure, did sufficient work for it to be launched and it was then towed to the Netherlands, where it was completed by van Goor and Spiekman at Zwartsluis in 1936. She was fitted with a diesel engine made by Humboldt-Deutzmotoren A.G. but the counter stern and the bridge amidships were features which betrayed her origin as a steam coaster. Farr mentions yet another hull building by Cocks, but no name or fate is known for this and it is assumed it was not far advanced and was simply dismantled. As there was only one building way, it is possible that the steel work had been fabricated but not erected.

Posthumous careers

Three of the coasters built by Cocks were acquired by James Fisher and Sons Ltd. of Barrow-in-Furness. Within a fortnight Orchis was sold by Fisher to owners in West Wales, but sank in 1935. Fisher traded the other pair until selling them to Brazilian owners. One was rebuilt as a motor vessel but the former Orleigh seems to have retained her Plenty steam engine until lost in 1963. The fourth steamer, Orenie,

Orenie, last of the coasters to be completed by Robert Cock and Sons Ltd., in the Richmond Dry Dock, probably just before her registration in April 1923. *[Cock Collection/North Devon Museum Trust]*

Orchis at Bristol with Walford Lines' funnel markings. *[J. and M. Clarkson]*

traded as *Rockville* until broken up in 1952, the only one of the original quartet not to meet a violent end. Yard number 187 had the longest career. Sold by her Dutch owners after only a year, she too went to South America.

The Cocks' shipyard itself was taken over by P.K. Harris and Sons. Philip K. Harris (1853-1938) had served an apprenticeship in Appledore as a ship's joiner, and had been to sea with Harrison Line. Coming ashore, with the help of his father-in-law he leased and later bought a small yard at Hubbastone in 1899. It could repair only small ships, but the business prospered sufficiently for Harris to purchase the adjoining New Quay Yard. With the yard's dry dock, Harris could now repair larger ships, and he even built one, the 130grt wooden schooner *P.T. Harris* of 1912. P.K. Harris never completed another sea-going vessel, and did not even fit out hull number 187 which he inherited from Cocks. However, the yard was used for fitting out vessels which had been launched by Hansen at Higher Cleavehouses, as described in 'Record' 14. Harris records that Hansen actually purchased the New Quay Yard in April 1920, considerably modernising it, only to sell the now much better equipped yard back to P.K. Harris at the same price five years later.

Hull number 187, left almost complete on Cocks' slipway at Appledore. *[North Devon Museum Trust]*

Harris continued to win repair work, his experience and reputation helping ensure that the Cock family could not break into this field. Although work was scarce in the 1930s, P.K. Harris took over Cocks' Richmond yard when the owning company was liquidated in 1932, a very bold move as to do so Harris had to mortgage his three yards, at New Quay, Hubbastone and Richmond Dry Dock. P.K. Harris died in 1938, but his sons built on the foundations he had laid to form a successful business and, unlike their father, they did fully embrace ship building. Their Appledore yards did much useful work with small craft during the Second World War, and went on to build tugs, trawlers and other specialised craft. Oddly, however,

P.K. Harris (Shipbuilders) Ltd. built no pure coasters, unlike the other North Devon builders, Cocks, Taw and Hansen.

Epitaph

With an output of just five and a half coasters plus a number of steel hulls for other small craft, the yard of Robert Cock and Sons Ltd. may seem a minor player in shipbuilding history. However, the company brought steel shipbuilding, not just to Appledore, but to North Devon. This was a local industry which – with some fits and restarts – survived longer than most yards on the Clyde, Tyne or Wear. The Cock family were held in high regard locally, according to Harris, who writes: 'I do not consider that this family's name has received the mention it so rightly deserves'.

Sailing and steam vessels built by James and Robert Cock and Sons

Until 1865, the builder was named as James Cock, then Robert Cock until 1897, and subsequently Robert Cock and Sons until 1906 when it became Robert Cock and Sons Ltd.. In addition to the vessels listed below, the Cocks built at least 15 wooden and 50 steel dumb barges.

Year	Name	Tons	Type/rig	Material	Yard
1855	Pomona	72	Polacca brigantine	Wood	Tavern
1858	Mary Boyns	116	Schooner	Wood	Tavern
1859	Louisa Jane	69	Schooner	Wood	Tavern
1861	Flying Scud/ Vacuna	130	Brigantine	Wood	Tavern
1863	Zampa	154	Schooner	Wood	Tavern
1864	Mela	93	Schooner	Wood	Tavern
1865	Charles Bath	19	Pilot boat	Wood	Tavern
1867	Eliza Sherris	196	Brigantine	Wood	Tavern
1869	Western Star	75	Schooner	Wood	Tavern
1870	Recruit	67	Schooner	Wood	Tavern
1872	Polly Mitchell	115	Schooner	Wood	Tavern
1875	Lizzie	33	Pilot boat	Wood	Tavern
1876	Maud	150	Schooner	Wood	Tavern
1879	M.A. Wilkinson	95	Schooner	Wood	Tavern
1885	Rosie	95	Schooner	Wood	?
1888	Florrie/ Message of Peace	51	Ketch	Wood	?
1890	Blazer	74	Ketch	Wood	?
1891	Ada	113	Schooner	Wood	?
1892	Florence	130	Schooner	Wood	?
1894	Clio	110	Brigantine	Wood	New Quay
1895	Dione	100	Schooner	Wood	New Quay
1896	Maud	120	Schooner	Wood	New Quay
1897	Sidney	112	Schooner	Wood	New Quay
1902	Madeliene	123	Schooner	Wood	Richmond
1903	Katie	124	Three-masted schooner	Wood	Richmond
1903	Norseman	126	Schooner	Wood	Richmond
1904	Ludham Castle	66	Steam drifter	Wood	Richmond
1904	Banshee	124	Schooner	Wood	Richmond
1904	Boy Billy	70	Steam drifter	Wood	Richmond
1904	Virginia	126	Schooner	Wood	Richmond
1904	Doris	137	Three-masted schooner	Steel	Iron
1904	Torridge/Viking/ Ternesund/Landan	158	Steam coaster	Steel	Iron
1905	A.M. Fox/Geraldo	125	Schooner	Wood	Richmond
1905	Rose	126	Three-masted schooner	Wood	Richmond
1906	Geisha	130	Three-masted schooner	Wood	Richmond
1906	Lucy Johns	144	Three-masted schooner	Steel	Iron
1906	Primrose	52	Steam tug	Steel	Iron
1906	Sun	130	Steam tug	Steel	Iron
1907	Provider	99	Steam trawler	Steel	Iron
1908	Roy	27	Steam tug	Steel	Iron
1908	Kipper	92	Steam trawler	Steel	Iron
1908	W.M.L.	145	Three-masted schooner	Steel	Iron
1909	Annie Reece/Diolinda	147	Three-masted schooner	Steel	Iron
1918	Orchis	483	Steam coaster	Steel	Iron
1919	Ortona/Stream Fisher/Guarara	482	Steam coaster	Steel	Iron
1919	Orleigh/Race Fisher/Guarahu/Tau	482	Steam coaster	Steel	Iron
1922	Orenie/Rockville	481	Steam coaster	Steel	Iron
1935	Ida Westers/Oriente/San Fernando/ Monagas/Bordaco	498	Motor coaster	Steel	Iron

Steam coasters built by Robert Cock and Sons Ltd., Appledore

TORRIDGE
O.N. 105245 158g 42n
96.9 x 19.3 x 9.1 feet
C. 2-cyl. by Crabtree and Co. Ltd., Great Yarmouth; 35 RHP.
1947: Oil engine 2-cyl. made in 1938 by Seffle Motorverkstad, Seffle, Sweden.
15.6.1904: Registered in the ownership of James H. Cock (32/64) and Frank G. Cock (32/64), Appledore as TORRIDGE
26.9.1906: Register closed on sale to Moss Aktiemöller, Moss, Norway and renamed VIKING.
1929: Sold to D/S Juno (Nils Rafen, manager), Holmstrand, Norway.
1940: Sold to Skibs A/S Ternesund (O. Börrresen, manager), Oslo, Norway and renamed TERNESUND.
1947: Converted to a motor vessel.
1948: Sold to N. Nielsen, Sœbövik, Norway

1950: Renamed LANDAN.
25.5.1953: Capsized and sank off Svaaholmen, south of Egersund, Norway, whilst on a voyage from Oslo to Trondheimfjord with general cargo.

183. ORCHIS
O.N. 135965 482g 204n
150.0 x 25.9 x 12.0 feet
T. 3-cyl. by Plenty and Son Ltd., Newbury; 113 NHP, 450 IHP, 9 knots.
2.1918: Completed for Robert Cock and Sons Ltd. (James H. Cocks, manager), Appledore as ORCHIS.
24.5.1932: Sold to James Fisher and Sons Ltd. (John Fisher, manager), Barrow-in-Furness.
3.6.1932: Sold to William Davies (32/64) and William G. James (32/64), Llangranog, Cardiganshire (William G. James and Sons, London, managers).
24.5.1935: Transferred to British Isles Coasters Ltd., Cardigan (William G. James,

Llangranog, manager).
30.11.1935: Foundered after springing a leak five miles south by west of Pencarrow Head, Cornwall whilst on a voyage from Par to Brixham, Dundee and Aberdeen with a cargo of china clay.
6.12.1935: Register closed.

184. ORTONA
O.N. 140856 483g 191n
150.0 x 25.7 x 12.0 feet
T. 3-cyl. by Plenty and Son Ltd., Newbury; 72 NHP, 450 IHP, 9 knots.
7.1949: Oil engine 8-cyl. 2SCSA made in 1946 by Fairbanks Morse and Company, Beloits, Wisconsin, U.S.A.
1.1919: Completed.
3.2.1919: Registered in the ownership of Robert Cock and Sons Ltd. (James H. Cocks, manager), Appledore as ORTONA.
24.5.1932: Sold to James Fisher and Sons Ltd., Barrow-in- Furness.
22.6.1932: Renamed STREAM FISHER.
2.1939: Sold to Empreza Internacional de Transports Ltda., Rio de Janeiro, Brazil and renamed GUARARA.
7.1949: Re-engined.
7.6.1954: Wrecked during a storm off Santa Catarina, Brazil and later sank.

185. WAR WHARFE/ORLEIGH
O.N. 140859 484g 199n
150.0 x 25.7 x 12.0 feet
T. 3-cyl. by Plenty and Son Ltd., Newbury; 72 NHP, 450 IHP, 9 knots.
28.7.1919: Launched.
12.1919: Completed.
1.12.1919: Registered in the ownership of Robert Cock and Sons Ltd. (James H. Cocks, manager), Appledore as ORLEIGH. She was ordered as WAR WHARFE by the Shipping Controller, London.
24.5.1932: Sold by mortgagees, National Provincial Bank Ltd., to James Fisher and Sons Ltd., Barrow-in-Furness.
18.6.1932: Renamed RACE FISHER.
2.1939: Sold to Empreza Internacional de Transports Ltda., Rio de Janeiro, Brazil and renamed GUARAHU.
1959: Sold to Wilfred Penha Borges, Santos, Brazil.
1960: Sold to Empreza de Navegacion Caillet Ltda., Paranagua, Brazil and renamed TAU.
1961: Sold to Oswaldo Pereira, Santos.
23.2.1963: Abandoned and sank in position 16.52 south, 39.80 west after springing a leak on grounding three miles south east of Punta Corumbau, Bahia Province, Brazil on 18.2.1963. She was on a voyage from Natal to Vitoria.

186. ORENIE
O.N. 144725 481g 189n
150.0 x 25.7 x 12.0 feet
T. 3-cyl. by Plenty and Son Ltd., Newbury; 71.6 NHP, 350 BHP, 450 IHP.
12.1922: Completed.
3.4.1923: Registered in the ownership

Upper: *Orchis* in Penzance, receiving attention to her funnel. *[Michael Guegan collection]*.
Lower: Yard number 184, *Ortona*, at Bristol. *[J. and M. Clarkson]*

Race Fisher (left), originally the *War Wharfe*, in the Thames on 20th June 1933. The coaster behind is the Newcastle owned *Bilton* (746/1920). *[Ships in Focus]*

Orenie (middle), yard number 186, was sold to John S. Monks and Co. Ltd. in 1932 after her mortgagees repossessed her. As *Rockville* (bottom), after the addition of a wheelhouse, emerging from Birkenhead Docks on to a busy River Mersey she gave her new Liverpool owners 20 years' service. *[National Maritime Museum P12212; Tom Rayner/J. and M. Clarkson]*

Hull 187, as *Bordaco*, at San Juan, Puerto Rico, on 30th May 1965. Interestingly, renaming as *Bordaco* is not recorded until 1992, exemplifying the difficulty for register book compilers of keeping track of small ships in Caribbean waters. *[William Schell]*

of Robert Cock and Sons Ltd. (James H. Cocks, manager), Appledore as ORENIE.
6.5.1932: Sold to John S. Monks and Co. Ltd., Liverpool by mortgagees.
28.5.1932: Renamed ROCKVILLE.
2.10.1952: Arrived at Barrow to be broken up by T.W. Ward Ltd. following partial demolition at Birkenhead.
22.1.1953: Register closed.

187. IDA WESTERS
498g 276n 149.8 x 26.3 x 11.9 feet
Oil engine 4SCSA 6-cyl. by Humboldt-Deutzmotoren A.G., Koln- Deutz, Germany.
Laid down by Robert Cock and Sons Ltd., Appledore.
15.10.1935: Launched after further work by P.K. Harris and Sons, Appledore.
1936: Completed by van Goor & Spiekman, Zwartsluis, Netherlands for J. Westers, Groningen, Netherlands as IDA WESTERS.
1937: Sold to Compania Anonima de Navegacion de Carenero, Caracas, Venezuela and renamed ORIENTE.
1944: Sold to Compania Anonima Venezolana de Navegacion, Caracas and renamed SAN FERNANDO.
1949: Renamed MONAGAS.
1954: Sold to Jesus Vicent Romero, La Guaira, Venezuela.
27.1.1983: Main engine broke down 39 miles south east of Cape Charles, Virginia, whilst on a voyage from Charleston to Baltimore. Subsequently towed to Norfolk, Virginia for repair.
By 1992: Sold to owners in the Dominican Republic. She was reportedly renamed BORDACO at this date, but there is

photographic evidence that she had already carried this name for some years.
15.9.1995: Deleted from 'Lloyd's Register' as continued existence in doubt.

Managed by James H. Cocks, Appledore

UALAN/ORPEN 1922-1927
O.N. 143491 492g 235n
155.4 x 25.0 x 10.3 feet
T. 3-cyl. by Gebroeder Stork, Hengelo; 43 NHP, 8 knots.
1935: Oil engine 6-cyl. 4SCSA by Motorenwerke Mannheim A.G., Mannheim, Germany.
5.1918: Completed by N.V. Scheepsbouwmaatschappij 'De Maas', Slikkerveer (Yard No. 1) for Rotterdam Algemeene Scheepvaart Maatschappij, Rotterdam, Netherlands as SLIKKERVEER.
1918: Sold to N.V. van der Eb en Dresselhuys Scheepvaart Maatschappij, Rotterdam, Netherlands.
15.11.1919: Registered in the ownership of the Enterprise Shipping Co. Ltd. (A.B. Clopet, manager), Cardiff and renamed UALAN.
21.10.1921: Sold to William Woodford, Leicester.
20.12.1921: Transferred to the Leicester Shipping Co. Ltd. (William Woodford, manager), Cardiff.
10.10.1922: Sold to George Rossiter, Topsham and William A. Holman, London (James H. Cocks, Appledore, manager).
28.8.1926: Transferred to Herbert Holman, London (James H. Cocks, Appledore, manager).

22.9.1926: Renamed ORPEN.
5.1927: Sold to Société Belge d'Armement Maritime S.A., Antwerp, Belgium and renamed MONA.
1931: Sold to Société Anonyme 'Fabrez' (D. Paniels, manager), Antwerp.
1932: Sold to N.V. Sleepschip Critias (D.J.L. Akkermans, manager), Bolnes, Netherlands and renamed LITTLE EVY.
1932: Sold to Bata a.s., Zlin, Czechoslovakia.
1935: Sold to Société Dunkerquoise du Cabotage (L Dewulf, managers), Dunkirk, France and renamed FRANCOIS TIXIER.
3.1935: Fitted with an oil engine.
19.8.1940: Taken over by the Ministry of Shipping, London (Alfred L. Duggan of Ald Shipping Co. Ltd., Bristol, manager).
1941: Owners became the Ministry of War Transport, London.
26.11.1941: Stranded in Ballyhalbert Bay, County Down whilst on a voyage from Glasgow to Sharpness with a cargo of tea.
23.8.1942: Refloated.
27.8.1942: Arrived in Belfast for dry docking.
1943: Converted to a salvage vessel and managers became the Liverpool and Glasgow Salvage Association, Liverpool.
20.11.1945: Returned to the ownership of Société Dunkerquoise du Cabotage (L Dewulf, managers), Dunkirk, France.
1947: Converted back to a cargo vessel.
8.7.1948: Capsized and sank off Sheringham in position 52.59.46 north, 01.11.05 east whilst on a voyage from Goole to Rouen with a cargo of coal.

MY PRESTON SHIPS AND I

John Clarkson

Friends ask how and when did I become interested in ships. My first thought is in the late 1950s when I started taking photographs of ships on the Ribble. However, my interest may have started much sooner, in 1947 to be exact. In September of that year Blue Funnel's *Theseus* (6,527/1908) was coming up the Ribble to Preston for scrapping when she broke adrift from her tugs and went aground on the marshes on the south side of the Ribble. She lay there for several weeks and there was much written about her in the local paper. My father took me down to Longton Marsh on the crossbar of his Raleigh bike to see the ship. She was a long way off but that was my first sight of a proper ship.

Up to 1952 we lived down a narrow, dismal road in Longton where my father had a poultry farm. He decided we should move to a larger smallholding and we went about four hundred yards on to the main road through the village and on the brow of the only higher ground for miles around. The house was an Edwardian semi-detached property with the usual ground and first floor but the surprise was it had two big attics, each with skylights which looked out towards the Ribble. I found by chance that I could just make out ships passing up and down the Ribble about three miles away. After a while I worked out that by looking at the tide-tables in the 'Lancashire Evening Post' I would have some idea of when ships may be passing. Also by looking at the same paper I could see what had gone up and down the river the previous day from the daily article 'Preston Shipping'. This reported arrivals and sailings on each tide of each day. This really fired up my interest.

Theseus ashore on the Ribble marshes. Whist inbound for Preston for scrapping in September 1947 she broke adrift and went aground. Due to the terrain it was almost impossible to get near to her. This photo was taken from Freckleton on the north bank of the Ribble. In late November Theseus was refloated by Glasgow tugs and delivered to Ward's yard. [World Ship Society Ltd.)

Another factor which contributed to my interest was that every Friday afternoon my parents and I went into Preston for the weekly shopping on the Ribble buses, some of them still with wooden seats. It's funny how the wooden seats stick in my mind - probably because they were so uncomfortable. If I was lucky we would go upstairs and sit on the left hand side of the bus going into town. If the bus went slowly over Penwortham Bridge there was just a chance to see what happened to be lying in Ward's shipbreaking yard. One ship which stood out clearly for a long time was Elders and Fyffes *Chirripo* (5,408/1920*)*. There was so much insulation in her and she had so many fires on board that it seemed to take years to scrap her. Sometimes, if the yard was busy and there was a ship awaiting scrapping, it

Preston Shipping

Arrivals.—January 17th, p.m. tide: Empire Cymric (2,300), Larne, vehicles; Ionic Ferry (1,160), Larne. vehicles; Empire Nordic (2,348), Larne vehicles: Meta (898), Gothenburg. general: Flut (248), Gruvon, timber. January 18th. a.m. tide: Nil. January 18th. p.m. tide: Clipper (315), Larne, containers: Oak (358), Newry. light; Shell Fitter (339), Heysham. fuel oil: Noach (326). Larne. containers: Esso Suwanee (105). Ellesmere Port. paraffin: Ballyduff (271). Larne. light; Craigolive (271), Belfast. general. January 19th. a.m. tide: Torridge Lass (178). Plymouth, clay. Ballyhaft (370). Larne. light.

Sailings.—January 17th. p.m. tide: Elisa (319), Larne. containers; Downshire (163). Coleraine, coal: Ballyhalbert (373), Belfast. coal. January 18th. a.m. tide: Nil. January 18th. p.m. tide: Empire Cymric (2,300). Larne, vehicles: Edgefield (273). Par. light; Ionic Ferry (1,160). Larne, vehicles: Goodwill (288). Larne. containers: Empire Nordic (2,348). Larne. vehicles: Authenticity (362). London, light. January 19th. a.m. tide: Noach (326). Larne. containers: Shell Fitter (339). Stanlow. light: Esso Suwanee (105), Stanlow light.

Vessels in Dock: Empire Gaelic, Empire Celtic, Hammonia, Ballydorn. Meta. Flut. Clipper Oak, Ballyduff. Craigolive, Torridge Lass. Ballyhaft.

Overseas vessels expected up to and including Monday. January 26th: Warma (1,030), Finnish: Sonja (867). Swedish: Robox (309). Dutch: Windward Islands (905). Swedish: Leeward Islands (910). Swedish: Enso (966) Finnish: Herta (184), Dutch: Forel (74). Dutch: Inspector Mellema (290). Dutch: I. W. Winck (1,299). Swedish: Jelva Dan (1,312). Danish: Hera (798). Swedish: Dalheim (2,747), Norwegian: Ramfosa (798). Norwegian.

Preston Shipping from the *Lancashire Evening Post*, of Monday, 19th January 1959. Monday's issues usually listed vessels expected from overseas during the coming week. In later years the article was renamed *In and Out of Preston Dock.*

Chirripo soon after her arrival at Preston for scrapping. *[Douglas B. Cochrane/World Ship Society Ltd.]*

would berth a little further up river, nearer to the bridge. My interest in shipbreaking was stimulated in the 1960s when Douglas Cochrane gave me a complete list of ships scrapped at Preston from 1894 and by Ken Brown of 'The Journal of Commerce' who supplied much additional information relating to the Preston yard and to other Ward yards.

All these factors helped to build up my interest. In 1958 I started biking down to Howick Cross, about a mile below the dock entrance, to photograph ships passing up or down the river using an old Box Brownie camera. I soon realised that the camera wasn't really up to the job and bought a cheap, second-hand 35mm camera but the results were still of little use. The next improvement was to go further downstream from Howick to where there were no electricity pylons. One could then take a better picture, better in that it had little background. I left school in the

summer of 1958 by which time a girl friend, Marion, had appeared on the scene. Soon after leaving school my father had died and any thoughts of going to sea melted away. I had various jobs in 1958 and 1959 but in December landed one on Preston Dock, working for Anglo Continental Container Services Ltd. Not a good job but I was there, working on Preston Docks. The Albert Edward Dock, to use its correct title, was a great place to work. Working relationships were good and just about everyone knew everyone else. If you needed help, or equipment, you were quickly pointed in the right direction. In the course of my travels around the dock I got to see, for the first time, copies of 'Lloyd's Register'. I could now research individual ships, check on their owners, tonnages, builders and previous names. After a time I managed to buy and scrounge old registers from various offices for reference at home – the start of my library. The

Noach (499/1952) was one of the first ships chartered by Anglo-Continental Container Services for their service to Larne. The scotch derrick is loading her on the regular berth - the North East Cross Berth in the basin. It is early days, her derricks have been removed but she is still light grey in colour. Later she was painted black and wore various funnel colours including those of Link Line and Coast Lines. A full cargo was about 26 containers including those on deck. The buildings behind her are the old cattle lairages later knocked down and replaced with a custom-built shed. Those to the left are timber sheds and were demolished to make parking areas for road vehicles. *[J. and M. Clarkson collection]*

following August I had an offer of a better position with Geest Industries Ltd. who ran a regular service, as regular as the tides at Preston would allow, out to the West Indies with general cargo and mainly bananas homewards. They had just taken delivery of two gas-turbine powered reefer ships, the *Geeststar* (1,927/1960) and *Geestland* (1,937/1960) and also used chartered tonnage, mainly Norwegian or German owned ships. I worked as a ship's agent and looked after both import and export cargo. The import cargo didn't take up much time as a full cargo of bananas was usually covered by two bills of lading and at the most three. Sometimes other fruits were carried, generally grapefruit and oranges, but from time to time all sorts of specialist foods imported by the local West Indian population living in Preston – tannias, dasheen, plantain and yams to name but a few.

As time went on the two owned ships became established and the masters started to employ West Indian crew members, signed on in the West Indies. These men arrived in the UK without seaman's papers which had to be obtained from the Dutch Consul in Liverpool. Passport-type photos were required; I obliged, and this became an important side-line to ship photography bringing in small amounts of cash to subsidise my ship photography.

The *Geestland* and *Geeststar* suffered many problems with the new type of engines which made much work returning damaged parts to Holland and bringing in replacements. Eventually the ships went back to Holland and were re-engined with diesels. After that we had few problems with them. The big difficulty at Preston was silting in the Ribble resulting in ships having to wait for bigger tides. With banana cargoes this was a problem and sometimes ships were diverted to other ports. Fleetwood and Liverpool were tried but ultimately Barry in South Wales became a regular port. As the number of sailings and size of ships used increased, Barry was favoured over Preston. As we had only a small staff in Barry some of us went down to Barry to assist.

The camera was still a problem and the next one was a Kodak Retinette, a popular camera at the time but still 35mm and still giving questionable results. A few words of advice

Geestland (1937/1960) (above) arriving at Preston and photographed from a point about two miles downstream from the dock. Here one could take photos from the top of the embankment, which gave more background, or from a narrow strip of marsh at the bottom. The *Geestdyk* (481/1961) (right), usually employed on the North Sea vegetable trade into Boston, was used for a period in 1968 to supply bananas to Ireland via Drogheda. The bananas were containerised as they were discharged from the ocean-going vessel.

The Geest ships, both owned and chartered, normally took two tugs. Seen at about the third mile is the chartered *Brunstal* (2,822/1959) in the care of *John* *Herbert* (146/1955) (ahead) and *Frank Jamieson* (146/1956). It was always good to see a decent sized ship coming in on a big tide as the resulting photographs had little clutter in the background. On the down side one had to get away quick after waiting for stern views to avoid a wetting from the ship's wash.

Geest's own *Geeststar* (1972/1960) (middle) and the chartered German-owned *Jogela* (500/1968) (right) at No.2 Shed in May 1969. It was unusual for us to have two ships in at the same time but this would have been due to a glut of bananas in the West Indies. On the left a Finnish ship, the *Pirjo* (1,923/1962), discharges pulp on to the Pulp Stage. Ward's yard is just to the left of the *Geeststar* under the bridge and the four chimneys were part of the local power station.

from a friend resulted in a further camera, an Ilford Sportsman. I made do with this and having films processed at the local chemist, when I could afford it, until 1963. By now Marion and I were married and living in Hutton. Cash was short to say the least. I was still taking photographs, developing the films myself but not having any printed. Our eldest daughter Julie was born in 1965 and followed by Joanne in 1968.

I had joined the Preston Branch of the World Ship Society in 1958 and became friends with Harry Stewart. Harry had been photographing ships at Preston on and off since 1925. In 1962 Alex Duncan was advertising to buy negatives and Harry told me he was contemplating selling his negative collection, both glass and film, which he had taken up to about 1960. To let such a collection leave Preston was unthinkable to me and a deal was struck whereby I would buy his collection – a few negatives at a time. To fund this I bought an old enlarger, complete with developing trays, and taught myself photographic printing, working on the floor in a spare bedroom. Patience was a virtue and in due course I was able to start making up photographic offers, mainly of

smaller vessels which often had not been photographed by the 'old school' of ship photographers.

In 1963 I was working mainly at Preston but occasionally at Barry and this brought me into contact with Des Harris of Penarth, well known then as 'Fotoship'. Des suggested that as I could now print from 6cm x 9cm negatives it was time to move up to a 6 x 9 camera. A Ross Ensign was suggested and the first of two was duly purchased. I remember well the first one. It was bought on a Friday straight after work and the only chance to try out the camera was on the early morning tide on the Saturday. I got up at about 5am and went off down the river and photographed the *Ben Maye* (323/1921) coming up river. The film was developed straight away. All was well and the camera did long and faithful service. In due course it was replaced with a Mamiya Press, later a Mamiya 6 x 7 and even later a further Press. The old Ensign, still in my possession, was sometimes put to use as a back-up or for colour slides of traction engines. All the 35mm negatives were, when short of funds, disposed of to finance various purchases.

An example of the work of Harry Stewart: the German-owned motor tanker *Mittelmeer* (6,370/1927). From the late 1920s through to the Second World War Preston was visited by many large - at that time - tankers bringing part cargoes of refined spirit from various oilfields. The tankers were discharged in the dock basin but on arrival or prior to sailing they had to pass through the locks into the dock, swing and then return through the locks to discharge or sail. Harry had his favourite places for photos, the Bull Nose - the most seaward point of the dock entrance, across the outer basin - where this photo was taken, and from the knuckle on the south side/landward end of the locks. *Mittelmeer* visited Preston only once, arriving on the 15th July 1929 from Port Arthur, Texas via Dublin, with a part cargo of motor spirit. Owned by John T. Essberger the *Mittelmeer* survived the war. She was taken in prize at Brunsbüttel in May 1945 and renamed *Empire Tagealand*. The following year she was allocated to Russia and renamed *Pamir*. [J. and M. Clarkson collection]

Ben Maye (323/1921) creeping up-river on a small tide on 1st September 1963. This photo was taken from an area of mud where Howick Brook joined the Ribble. The stones in the foreground have been placed to reduce erosion. The early morning light brings up more detail in the sky and on some parts of the ship. She was followed by the *Trinitas* (499/1951), the negative of which has sadly been used in an exchange.

My better Preston photos, in my own opinion, were generally taken at weekends from various places down the river rather than on the dock estate. Pictures taken on the dock were interesting in that often one could see what other ships were in port at the time. Movements in working hours were captured by thinking up excuses to get out of the office, on to my trusty stead and off around the dock. Lunch-times were useful when the tides were at suitable times but again pictures were mainly taken in the dock and rapid rides down the river were only made in exceptional cases and when a good excuse was available for not getting back into the office on time. A good instance of a long lunch-hour was when the *Marie Lamey* (208/1922) and *Irene Lamey* (192/1915)

arrived for breaking up. High water was about 13.30 hours and to be sure I left the office at 12, riding through the outskirts of Preston and off down the river to meet them as far downstream as possible. I went to something like the three-mile marker and could see them in the distance making slow progress with the tide behind them. I wasn't going to miss the opportunity of photographing two ships arriving together for scrapping so waited, and waited. Slowly they came up to me, *Irene*, well and truly worn out, towing the *Marie*. The harbour master must have realised there was a problem and sent one of the Preston tugs to assist as by now the tide had turned and progress became even slower. To cut a long story short I crept back into work, very quietly, at well

The *Irene Lamey* (192/1915) (right) and *Marie Lamey* (208/1922) approaching the dock entrance where they will veer to starboard

and go up the New Diversion to Ward's yard. The New Diversion is so named as when the dock was built the Ribble had to be diverted

into a newly-dug channel. I rarely took pictures so close to the dock as several electric lines crossed the river via pairs of large pylons.

Over the years timber and pulp were amongst the biggest commodities handled at Preston. Above the Norwegian *Lindborg* (1,519/1929) comes up-river with a timber cargo. Despite the good working relationships enjoyed

at Preston the discharge of this cargo did not go well. The ship's very small hatches slowed down discharge and the dockers asked for more pay. The result was a prolonged strike which was not good for Preston. In due course she

completed discharge during which time stout timbers, almost up to bridge level, were erected along her bulwarks, wire netting was strung between them and she loaded a cargo of coke for Norway.

The British-built, Finnish-owned *Amra* (2,353/1946) is seen about three miles from Preston inbound with a cargo of wood pulp. The day started off very foggy but cleared just in time. It is very near to high water and the lack of wind is emphasised by the reflection in the water.

after 3pm with a couple of exposed films in my pocket. Over the following months I often visited the yard, only about 100 yards from work across the railway sidings, photographing the tugs as they were demolished.

Buying Harry Stewart's collection made me think about buying other collections to build up a good negative archive. Various small collections were purchased the most unusual of which was one of about 150 postcard-sized glass plates dating back to 1908 and 1910. In 1984 the first big collection came along, that of B. and A. Feilden of Birkdale, Southport. The price was beyond my means but with the help of a third party, paid back with prints, the collection was bought, cleaned up, re-bagged and catalogued. In the early 1980s when Des Harris was not well he sold his collection in bits and pieces. I took some parts but sadly the best went to a collector in New Zealand. The biggest collection purchased was that of Tom Rayner on the Isle of Wight. This included the negatives of John McRoberts taken on Merseyside. The negatives of a professional photographer at Hull and part of the accumulation of negatives taken by Barnard and Straker on the Humber in the early 1900s were also added in the 1990s. Later Norman Taylor offered me the coaster and tramp steamer plates from the 'Bristol Series' taken at Bristol and Avonmouth. Negatives were bought from Peter Foxley out in Malaya and from photographers nearer home. Many more were added through exchanges. One regret was not getting hold of Douglas Cochrane's collection which went to the World Ship Society. This would have complemented the negatives of Harry Stewart. Harry was never a wealthy man and when on hard times in the 1930s was unable to spend money on materials for a number of years. Douglas was in regular employment at County Hall throughout the depression.

Most of my photography at Preston was done in the 1960s. I passed my driving test in 1968 so that when Geest closed their Preston office I would be in a position to work elsewhere. The office closed at the end of 1970 and I

The postcard-size plates were mainly of British owned ships and are thought to have been taken in 1908 and 1910. The *Helen Craig* (417/1891) was built by Workman, Clark and Co.Ltd., Belfast for Hugh Craig, also of Belfast. In her early years she was an infrequent visitor to Preston but from 1909 she became a regular caller, usually making one round voyage each week with coal or general cargo. *Helen Craig* had a long life, her last departure from Preston was on 19th November 1959 for Belfast and then on to Haulbowline for breaking up. *[J. and M. Clarkson collection]*

went to James Fisher in Liverpool as a ship's agent, covering Liverpool, Manchester and various places on the Ship Canal. I always carried my camera with me. Marion and I, having two children, found that spare time was a very valuable commodity and although there was little to spare I still managed a few photographs at Preston but only at weekends. In 1972 I left Fishers and returned to Preston to work for a small shipping and forwarding agency. The work was mainly imports and exports but we acted as agents for a few ships.

Shipping at Preston was now decreasing; Geest had gone, and the last Atlantic Steam Navigation ro-ro ferry sailed on 30th June 1974 although they continued to use Preston for lift-on/lift-off containers. Shell and Esso closed their depots leaving only Lancashire Tar, importers of tar and exporters of pitch, and Globe Petroleum, who bought petrol mainly on the Continent for distribution to their garages in

Throughout the life of the dock coal was an important commodity. Most of the time it was for export, mainly to Northern Ireland. At other times, for example during the 1926 general strike, it was imported in large quantities. John Kelly Ltd. of Belfast probably took out most coal but the ships of Hugh Craig of Belfast, Fishers of Newry, Rainey of Londonderry and Coes of Liverpool to name a few were frequent visitors. Built at Glasgow the *Ballygarvey* (662/1937) (above) was Kelly's last steamer. Metcalf's tanker *Peter M* (972/1937) is in the background on the north side of the basin. In due course the steamers were replaced with motor ships such as the *Ballyloran* (1,092/1958) (right). The first of the pylons down the river which spoiled so many photos can be seen to the left.

In May 1948 the Atlantic Steam Navigation Co. Ltd. started a ro-ro service between Preston and Larne using surplus war-built landing craft. The ships were *Empire Cedric* (4,291/1945), *Empire Doric* (4,291/1945) and *Empire Gaelic* (4,291/1945). All gave good service and were joined by the *Empire Cymric* (4,291/1945) in 1955 and *Empire Nordic* (4,295/1945) (top) in 1956. Later ships were specially built for the service, the *Bardic Ferry (2,550/1957)* (right) and *Ionic Ferry* (2,557/1958). *Bardic Ferry* made the final ro-ro sailing for Atlantic Steam Navigation from Preston on 30th June 1974. From July 1966 until October 1967 a US-built landing craft, the *Baltic Ferry* (1,909/1945) (bottom) was employed. Other ferries, similar to, but larger than the *Bardic Ferry* and *Ionic Ferry* were built. The first was the *Cerdic Ferry* (2,455/1961) which came to Preston to relieve for dry dockings. The second was the *Doric Ferry* (2,573/1962) used on the owner's Belfast service.

In the late sixties Atlantic Steam Navigation took on charter two Dutch-built ships owned by Fishers of Barrow, the *Orwell Fisher* (1,374/1968) and *Solway Fisher* (1,374/1968) (opposite page, top) for their container services to Ireland. Over the following twelve years the *Solway Fisher* visited Preston over 600 times. In the same period the *Orwell Fisher* made exactly 900 trips, sailing from Preston for the last time on 29th

June 1980. In this photo, taken on 30th April 1974, the *Solway Fisher* is using what was one of the ro-ro ferry berths, the bridge and pontoon having been removed.

Chartered at the same time were two German owned vessels, *Barbel Bolten* (1,374/1968) (middle) and *Marietta Bolten* (999/1968). The *Marietta* was renamed *Hermia* in 1974 and continued to serve at Preston until February 1978.

Atlantic Steam Navigation were not the only company to use Preston for container traffic. Many others came and went such as Coast Lines, Link Line, Greenore Ferry Services, Ronagency and Anglo-Irish Transport. United States Lines and P. & O. used Preston occasionally when they had problems elsewhere.

In 1972 the US-owned Sealand Containers started using Preston for a feeder service to their deep-sea terminal in Rotterdam. The main ship on the service was the *Black Swan* (994/1969) (bottom). At first the port's scotch derricks were used for cargo handling. A Liebherr gantry crane was purchased and erected on the New Berth in 1972 for the service, however, due to labour problems it was not used until 1973. The *Black Swan*, originally 97.16 metres long was lengthened to 121.54 metres in 1976 and renamed *ASD Black Swan*. It was a bad day for Preston when Sealand withdrew in November 1977. The crane was sold after the dock closed, dismantled and shipped to Greenore, Ireland.

In the 1970s there was a distinct shortage of ware potatoes in the United Kingdom. To fill the gap potatoes were imported from Eastern Mediterranean countries. The season would start in February with imports from Egypt, later cargoes coming from Cyprus and the final ones in May from Malaga in Spain. The Egypt and Cyprus consignments often came in older, more interesting vessels such as the *Pergamos* (1,594/1949) (above) seen coming up-river on 5th March 1976. The cargoes were labour intensive and often caused delays to other ships. The condition of the potatoes on arrival could vary from very good to very bad, one of the last cargoes having to be taken out of the ship by grabs.

From time to time part cargoes of good quality wood pulp came in from the West Coast of the U.S.A. The cargoes were carried in 'big' ships for Preston such as the pre-war German-owned *Hein Hoyer* (5,976/1937) (below) which arrived on 20th February 1964 with 2,321 tons from Long View, U.S.A. via Liverpool and Garston. She was 464 feet in length - long for Preston.

The last Esso tanker to bring petrol and other fuel oils was the *Esso Caernarvon* (right) seen sailing from Preston for the final time in June 1973.

No dock was without its tragedies. The Russian timber-carrier *Igarkales* (2,902/1962) (below) arrived on 24th September 1964 with a full cargo of timber from Igarka, Northern Russia. There was a fire onboard one night and one crew member died. The Russian diesel-electric salvage tug *Hermes* (828/1962) arrived on the 18th October from Rostock and the pair of them sailed for Leningrad on 21st October.

the North West. Pulp and timber shipments were decreasing as the importers were finding it more economical to use East Coast ports and road transport. Dredging was stopped to save money, the sand pumps disposed of and in due course the decision was taken in 1976 to close the port. The last commercial cargo was pulp, brought in by the Japanese-built *Sea Rhine* (1,475/1978) on 16th October 1981 although *Hoveringham V* (1,027/1969) discharged a cargo of sand a few days later. As trade decreased so did my photography at Preston. In the late 1970s the agency I was working for left their dock premises and moved a few miles out of Preston virtually bringing to an end my photography of ships at Preston. After closure it was at least ten years before I ventured on to the redeveloped dock estate.

More photography was now done at other North West ports and at Goole. I especially liked Goole as the ships were mainly of a similar size and type to what had been

at Preston. After a brief visit to Holland with Des Harris in 1984 I made a few annual trips to Holland and one year included a visit to the Kiel Canal. By the late 1990s I had more or less stopped taking photographs and concentrated on printing from my negative collection and on Ships in Focus, set up with Roy Fenton in 1994.

So where are we now? Ships or no ships Marion and I are still together. The girls have moved on and we now have eight grandchildren ranging from 20 down to 11 years of age The negative collection is often used to illustrate articles in 'Record' and in our other publications. I no longer do 'wet' printing but from time to time supply digital prints. There is still a stock of postcards tucked away in what was the darkroom and hopefully before too long a start will be made in disposing of them, or at least in reducing them. As to the future there are several books in the pipeline and hopefully 'Record' will continue into the foreseeable future.

The motor ship *Aba* had an extraordinary career. She was ordered from Barclay, Curle and Co. Ltd. by the Imperial Russian Government but, by the time of her completion in September 1918, Russia had been through a revolution, and she was delivered to Glen Line Ltd. as *Glenapp*. In 1920 she was transferred within the Kylsant Group to British and African Steam Navigation Co. Ltd., and rebuilt with passenger accommodation, being renamed *Aba* in October 1921. She was requisitioned to become a hospital ship at the very beginning of the Second World War, but her sanctity was compromised twice. In May 1941 she was bombed off Crete, and in March 1944 again attacked by the Luftwaffe in Naples. Three months after being returned to owners (now Elder Dempster Lines Ltd.) in January 1947, *Aba* was sold to the Bawtry Steamship Co. Ltd., London, a company controlled by George J. Livanos, and later renamed *Matrona*. As recorded in the text, she capsized in Birkenhead Docks on 30th October 1947. She was righted in June 1948, but was now completely beyond use, and arrived at Barrow for breaking up by T.W. Ward Ltd. in October 1948.

The photographs were taken at Funchal (with a black hull) and at Dartmouth on 9th December 1931 (grey hull). *[Renato A.M. Santo/Roy Fenton collection; Laurence Dunn/Ships in Focus]*

ELDER DEMPSTER POST WAR PART 4: THE MAIL BOATS

Andrew Bell

No record of the development of the Elder Dempster fleet after 1945 would be complete without mention of the passenger ships widely known as the mail boats. In many ways they were a service that many interested in passenger ships ignored for they ran on an unglamorous route providing the type of service that was taken for granted. By the time victory in Europe was complete in May 1945 only the oldest passenger ship in the fleet remained. The 7,347gt *Aba* had come into Elder Dempster's service in 1921 as the world's first ocean-going diesel-engined passenger ship. Elderly by 1939, she was a worn-out hospital ship by the end of the war and, in 1947, was sold to Greek buyers who, ignoring the seller's advice, compromised the ship's stability, and, renamed the *Matrona,* she disobligingly capsized in Bidston Dock, Birkenhead (see photograph in 'Record' 3, pages 150-1).

The extent of Elder Dempster's war losses resulted in priority being given to obtaining Admiralty licences to build, and in February 1945 two berths for new buildings were reserved with Vickers-Armstrong at Barrow-in-Furness. The design of this pair closely followed that of the *Abosso* (11,330/1935) with a capacity for 269 passengers in two classes and - almost as importantly - for 3,000 tonnes of general cargo. The evolution of the design was apparent with the replacement of a large airy 'Palm Court' at the after end of the Boat Deck by a full-size open-air swimming pool and adjacent sun deck. All the first class cabins had en-suite showers but, curiously, no toilets. What machinery was available dictated that two four-cylinder opposed-piston Doxfords provided the uncomplicated main engines, giving a service speed of 15½ knots from a power output of 9,450 BHP. The dumpy profile of the *Accra* and the *Apapa* is attributed to a lack of steel available at the economically fraught times in which they were constructed. However, their length overall was not less than the four similar ships built between 1926 and 1935. The elimination of the forward well deck, so that unberthed inter-West African-coastal passengers were sheltered from tropical rain, contributed to the vessels' big-hull look. The squat funnel and the over-tall masts did not help and this was one reason why, although their hull colours were changed from the original black to light grey, they were never repainted white under Elder Dempster's ownership. A loaded draught of 25 feet 6 inches enabled them to sail fully loaded homeward bound from Lagos.

The *Accra* came into service on 24th September 1947 and, when followed by her sister ship *Apapa* in March 1948, a scheduled sailing every three weeks between Liverpool, Las Palmas, Freetown, Takoradi and Lagos was re-established. The ships' service speed was 15 knots but 16 knots could be maintained if necessary. It was always intended that a third mail boat be built and the contract went, in March 1949, to Alexander Stephens on the Clyde who sought to re-establish their reputation for building passenger ships.

Completed by Cammell Laird and Co. Ltd. at Birkenhead in October 1935, *Abosso* was Elder Dempster's flag ship for just seven years. On 29th October 1942 she was torpedoed by *U 575* whilst sailing alone, homeward bound from Cape Town. Losses were horrendous: 172 out of 186 passengers (mostly troops) and 168 of the 182 crew. *[B. and A. Feilden/J. and M. Clarkson]*

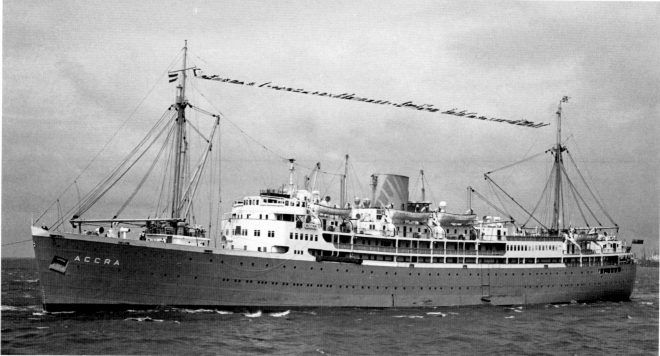

Accra is first seen (top) on Princes' Landing Stage, Liverpool at the comencement of her maiden voyage on 24th September 1947 with her original black hull.

The more familiar grey hull is evident in the other two photographs, that in the middle taken in the early 1960s.

Accra went straight from Elder Dempster service to the breakers, sailing from Liverpool on 13th November 1967 to Cartagena, where she was broken up by J. Navarro Frances.
[John McRoberts/J.and M. Clarkson; J. and M. Clarkson; Ships in Focus]

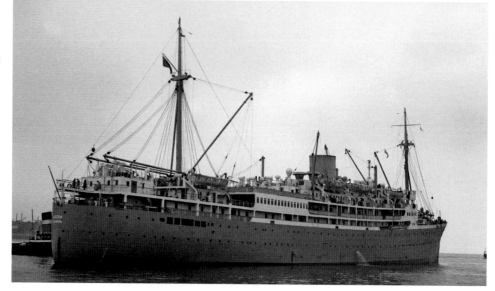

Unlike her sister, *Apapa* went on to have a further career. Sold to Shun Cheong Steam Navigation Co. Ltd. of Hong Kong in November 1968 she was renamed *Taipooshan* (bottom). She was sold for demolition to Yun Shen Steel and Iron Works at Kaohsiung in February 1975.

The inspired *Aureol*

If ever there was a design that started from a clean sheet of paper it was that of the *Aureol*. Even the name, originating from the mountain that dominates Freetown in Sierra Leone and suggested by a passenger, had never been used before. The passengers were accommodated in two classes – 269 in first and 76 in cabin class – the latter a much re-vamped second class that occupied the after end of the Lower Promenade B Deck, and was laid out similarly to that of three Lloyd Triestino ships built at the same time for the Italy to Australia service. In this self-contained structure the cabin class passengers had public rooms that were as, if not more, attractive than the first class facilities further forward at the same level: Number 3 hatchway divided the two. For the cabin class there was a spacious smoke room, a small but much-used cocktail bar, a library and a large lounge with full width sliding doors that opened out on to deck space overlooking the stern.

For the first class the midships area stretching forward to Number 2 hatchway was taken up by a group of four public rooms serving the usual purposes. Of these the Library – later turned into a cinema – was the most attractive. Although the Dining Saloon, with its capacity to seat 268 passengers and the senior officers in one sitting, was air conditioned, the rest of the *Aureol* was designed around being as airy as possible in the tropics, for 24 days out of the 32-day round voyage might be spent in hot weather. This could best be seen in most of the first class cabins – all of which were outside – each having two large portholes. The most unusual feature of all was a large covered deck space on to which the Main Lounge opened at the forward end of B. Deck. Accessed through the ubiquitous Essavian folding screens, this space was intended for outdoor living and repeated a feature on all of the large pre-Second World War mail boats. It was never much used and after the *Aureol*

had air conditioning installed throughout it became wasted, unused space. Despite bursts of imagination as to what to do with it coming and going, it remained as-built until the end of the ship's career.

The *Aureol's* passenger cabins were disappointing. It was as though all the practical inspiration that had been used to design a step-changing mail boat had run dry by the time it came to the layout of the first class cabins. The twin-bedded cabins had one berth fore-and-aft along the ship's side and the other athwartships. Little attempt was made to create appealing décor - each cabin had a private lavatory but no shower - they and the baths were a communal facility. The exception to this were the four very special suites which were sited right across the forward end of A Deck. By clever design four suites could be converted into a pair, each of which then had a bedroom, two bath rooms, a sitting room and a delightful windowed veranda from which there was an all-round view over the bow. They were the show piece of the ship, seldom unbooked on any voyage the *Aureol* made.

Before the Second World War most of West Africa was still considered too unhealthy a place to bring up European children. With public health much improved by colonial development and the threat of malaria containable, Elder Dempster realised that expatriate families would now travel in considerable numbers. In the highest level of accommodation – one deck below bridge level – the *Aureol* had a specific area assigned for children: in its space and facilities it rivalled that of any ship afloat. It equalled even that on board Shaw Savill's flagship *Dominion Monarch* (26,463/1939) for it comprised a large play room that opened on to a deck with its own paddling pool and sand pit. There was a small dining saloon and even miniaturised toilets. Two nursery nurses were in attendance. At the after end of the A Deck just below the children's facilities was a large swimming pool adjacent to a veranda bar that, at night

Aureol on Princes' Landing Stage. *[John McRoberts/J. and M. Clarkson]*

with the curtains drawn, became a stylish space in which to socialise.

Unseen by the passengers within her interior the *Aureol* had another practical feature that served her well, the working alleyway that ran the length of the ship on D Deck. From this alleyway could be accessed the engine room with its two Doxford main engines (producing a total of 9,400 BHP), all four cargo hatches, the main galley and much of the ship's support services. After leaving Liverpool the mail boat service called at Las Palmas for fuel, Freetown, Takoradi and Lagos: at all these ports the working alleyway proved its use by keeping stevedore labour off the passenger decks. This also applied during the ten-day turn round in Liverpool and the six-day one in Lagos. Although seemingly lavish, it ensured that a maintenance programme could be progressed and the mail boats were seldom taken out of service during the whole of their histories – even dry docking in Liverpool could be fitted in, plus a phased installation of air conditioning and an increase in refrigerated cargo space.

The credit for what became the *Aureol's* enduringly successful design goes to J.A. Waddington who had become the company's own naval architect in 1920. He had translated the vision of a trio of directors led by the chairman John H. Joyce which inspired Malcolm Bruce Glasier and Allan Bennett, respectively the ship's husband and technical director. J.A. Waddington is remembered as 'a kindly man with a serene outlook on life'. In the Alexander Stephens' archive at Glasgow University is much of the correspondence between the builders and the owners in Liverpool. It records a time of desperate shortages of everything, but in particular, steel: any quality steel from any source. At times the yard was receiving only 25% of the steel that they needed. Britain's post-Second World War near-bankruptcy, the reconstruction of bomb-damaged towns and cities but above all the drive to earn foreign currency – almost anyone's currency – resulted in the much-needed third mail boat being on the building berth for 18 months between keel laying and her launch in March 1951. In Mrs Tansley

The yacht-like *Aureol* (above). Despite her deteriorating steelwork, she had an extended, if sedentary, further career after being retired by Elder Dempster in 1974. Renamed *Marianna VI* under the Panama flag by John S. Latsis, she was used as an accommodation ship at Jeddah and elsewhere. Retired to Eleusis (where the photograph on the right was taken in October 1999), she was not broken up until 2001, arriving at Alang on 5th June to be dealt with by Arya Ship Breaking (P), Ltd. *[J. and M. Clarkson; Roy Fenton collection]*

the choice of sponsor was made as a solid tactical business decision: Mr (later Sir) Eric Tansley was the chairman of the West African Produce Marketing Board which used the British Conference lines to carry the three colonies' tropical produce. With the exception of the Crown Agents based in London, who were the source of much southbound cargo and passenger bookings, no commercial customer/shipper was more important than Tansley's Marketing Board.

Although launched with the same light grey hull as the *Accra* and the *Apapa* (and incorporating a yellow cheat-line), the hull was changed to white during the months she was fitting out afloat. The *Aureol's* fine lines emphasised her clipper bow, graceful sheer and spoon-shaped stern. Another change from the original design was that the two conventional masts were replaced by one tripod mast located aft of the Bridge: the result was a visual triumph that gave much pleasure to many for years to come. With the first phase of the acceptance trials over, the *Aureol* loaded a full general cargo in Liverpool for West Africa and headed back to the Firth of Clyde with a guest list of passengers. They had much to celebrate ahead of the first fare paying passengers embarked at Princes Landing Stage, Liverpool when the *Aureol* set off on her maiden voyage on 9th November 1951.

With the delivery of the *Aureol* began a fortnightly service to the main ports of Commonwealth West Africa with Lagos being reached in 12 days. When in their home port of Liverpool, the mail boats were almost adjacent to Elder Dempster's head office in India Buildings, Water Street. At their designated berth in Canada Dock they were ten minutes away by car: alongside the Landing Stage on Mondays (arriving) or Fridays (sailing) – just a five-minute walk away. General cargoes were a vital part of the mail boats' revenue. The freight rates were not surcharged but the ships were allocated all the high-paying commodities. Southbound, there were cars (although, frustratingly, there was a limitation on numbers); Guinness in tanks going to their brewery at Lagos; textiles; specie – coins and currency; machinery;

supermarket stocks; letter and parcel mail and, for bottom weight, bagged salt in pure white bags from ICI. The most unpopular cargo of all was carbon black for Dunlop's Nigerian tyre-making plant. Northbound there was tropical produce comprising oil seeds and baled cotton, and all the tin produced in ingot form from Jos in Nigeria. Refrigerated foodstuffs were carried both ways: southbound they were for city supermarkets whilst northbound there were tropical foodstuffs for the U.K.'s growing Afro-Caribbean markets.

The London mail boats

A 1957 episode personified the agile profitability with which Elder Dempster was run in the time of the chairmanship of John H. Joyce. The growth of the South East, centred on London as a source of consumer goods' exports, had been one of the post-Second World War phenomena. Tilbury was becoming as much a part of trade with West Africa as Liverpool had been during previous generations. Two of the staple items out of the Thames were bagged Blue Circle cement from just across the river at Gravesend and Ford cars assembled at Dagenham. Although titled an assistant manager, John H. Joyce's aide was much more and proved to be one of the most outstanding up-and-coming shipping men of those who had returned from war service and were driving towards creating peace and prosperity. Donald Tod masterminded a merging of opportunities. In 1957, the Cayzer clan, in a rationalising mode having at last successfully taken over Union Castle, closed down Bullard King and with it made redundant two passenger cargo ships built in the 1930s. Donald Tod saw an opening for them - filling their four lower holds with bagged cement for Lagos and their 'tween decks with Ford's export range of cars, and northbound with tropical produce, much of it lifted out of the Niger Delta ports by Elder Dempster's feeder service coasters. Here was realised that dream of any cargo liner man, a shipping service between two terminal ports. The bonus that went with this opportunistic used-ship

Photographed on the Thames, *Calabar* (the fourth of the name, taken from a river and trading station in Nigeria) was built in 1936 by Swan, Hunter and Wigham Richardson Ltd. for Bullard, King and Co. Ltd. as *Umtali*. *Calabar* went to Inverkeithing for demolition in January 1963. *[Ships in Focus]*

A sister to *Calabar*, *Winneba* was completed at the same Tyneside yard almost two years later as *Umgeni*. The second of the name, taken from a surf port in what is now Ghana, *Winneba* was sold to Antwerp breakers in January 1963. The photograph to the right was taken in May 1961, that below in June 1960. *[J. and M. Clarkson; Ships in Focus]*

purchase was that the *Umgeni* (8,180/1938) and the *Umtali* (8,162/1936), duly renamed *Winneba* and *Calabar*, could each carry 105 passengers in a grade of accommodation that was described by Claude Boswell, the revolutionary fleet catering manager, as being just like 'fading Victorian seaside boarding houses'. But he ensured that the standard of their service was high and, for a segment of the market, they soon became very popular.

The Port of London Authority had built for P&O – Orient Lines a handsome passenger terminal in the north west corner of Tilbury Dock: it supplemented the famous riverside Landing Stage but was seldom used. Elder Dempster were happy to do so, giving their passengers the facilities of one of the most modern terminals in the country. In contrast, passengers joining or leaving the Liverpool mail boats were subjected to the basic facilities of Princes Landing Stage at the Pierhead; so rustic were they that they

at least encouraged a fast transit. Until 1968, with so many passengers originating from or heading for London and the South East, on sailing day a boat train was run from Euston (departing at 10.00 hours) to Liverpool Riverside Station which reached the adjacent Landing Stage by a circuitous route through the northern suburbs of Liverpool; on the last sector across the Dock Road it being preceded by a man with a red flag. The boat train was scheduled on an inducement basis, if required, to serve inward mail boats on a Monday morning. The station which had been built at the Tilbury Dock passenger terminal was never used for the London mail boats.

In both directions the London mail boats were routed via Madeira and Freetown and on their monthly schedule ran for five years before they were sold for scrap in 1963. Fortune had favoured the bold and the pair had returned a handsome profit.

Eket approaching Calabar (left) and *Oron* berthed at Calabar (right). *[Derek Bailey]*

Calabar ferries

There was another Elder Dempster passenger fleet that deserves more prominence than it has had in the company's documented history: the Calabar Ferry Service that carried 500,000 passengers a year. It was in reality a miniature mail boat service providing a vital link between the principal towns in a riverene setting in Eastern Nigeria and the rest of the Federation. The route was 16-miles long taking an hour and a half seawards down the Calabar River, across the Parrot Island shallows and up the Cross River to Oron. Three ships made up the fleet: *Oron* (277/1938), *Itu* (129/1954) and the flagship *Eket* (394/1950). They were in the Elder Dempster colours and flew their houseflag: even the biscuits sold on board came from Huntley and Palmers. From the outset in 1920, when G.H. Avezathe, the long-serving local branch manager, founded the service, the ferries were manned and commanded by Nigerian seamen a few of whom were carefully promoted to 'river masters'. Both the *Oron* and the *Eket* were built to carry vehicles and cargo: the *Itu* was designed for a service up the Cross River that soon proved unprofitable so she took the off-peak sailings of the main ferry service. At Calabar there was a self-contained support organization that comprised an engineering base, a dry dock, a ro-ro landing stage that had been built and used for the Normandy Landings in 1944 (recovered and sold on), and onshore passenger facilities. Managed by a small team of four British expatriates, the service was embarrassingly profitable. Sold to the regional South East State government in 1974, it ceased several years later when it was no longer needed thanks to an extensive road building programme.

End of the mail boats

So important was the mail boat service to Elder Dempster that between 1951 and 1974 there was, in the naval architects' collection of projected ships, an updated design for the next mail boat. One of them, glimpsed by your author in 1958, was a junior version of Shaw Savill's trend-setting *Southern Cross* (20,204/1955). Several factors put paid to replacements of the *Accra* in 1967 and the *Apapa* in 1968. The outbreak of a secessionist civil war (1967-1970) jeopardised the stable future of a prosperous Nigeria that had become independent in 1960, whilst jet airliners had shrunk the flying time between London and Lagos to just over six hours with the transit over the Sahara no longer a major challenge to aviation. By 1968 Elder Dempster had

been integrated into the Ocean Group that had originally comprised Alfred Holt's Blue Funnel Line and which had no record of taking passenger carrying seriously (nevertheless, their archives show that, in 1972, the acquisition of Cunard's laid up *Carinthia* (21,947/1956) and *Franconia* (22,637/1955) was assessed in detail with the intention of getting into full-time, world cruising).

In 1973 *Aureol* was lying at the passenger ship terminal at Lagos' Apapa quay when a mishandled Nigerian National Line ship swinging into a flood tide struck her a glancing blow amidships at C Deck level. To assess the damage, bulkheads were taken down in a group of port side passenger cabins. For the first time in 22 years the *Aureol's* interior steel work was on view: such was the extent of the corrosion that it was apparent that the wasting away of inferior quality steel was a major problem. The move of her UK terminal port from Liverpool to Southampton in 1972 had not been a success because the voyages' revenue was not underpinned by the fortnightly general cargo service that still flourished from Liverpool.

With the *Aureol* scheduled to be taken out of service in late 1974 there was one last project that might have replaced her. In December 1973 an assessment team from Liverpool flew to the Far East to view the Swire Group's *Coral Princess* (9,696/1962). She had been bought to operate cruises for honeymooning Japanese in 1970. In 1973 Swire's China Navigation Company was 50% owned by Ocean, thus an offset transfer between fleets could have been made. The assessors' conclusions were entirely negative. The *Coral Princess* had a quirky electrical system that needed replacing. Another problem was the arrangement of the passenger cabins; each shared one bathroom between two cabins.

Was an inheritance abandoned? Your author considers it was. Elder Dempster had successfully handled the changing passenger traffic flow. The mail boat service came to be professionally marketed with the southbound trade being used by West Africans returning from Europe, well laden with goods and luggage. Northbound expatriates started holidays in style but without hassle and accompanied by their cars. Round voyages on a working cargo-passenger ship were becoming well known and recommended. Short cruises based on Lagos were a sell out, and of course there was the flourishing inter-West African-coastal traffic which was governed by mysterious movements of accompanied trade goods as diverse as textiles and betelnuts. The besetting and ignored problem was that in a fast changing era Elder Dempster were operating long-haul ships on a short-haul trade. The roll-on roll-off revolution and what came to be known as ro-pax was becoming established. Had a foresighted Ocean Group management done a deal with Swedish owners and German shipbuilders to acquire ships similar to the *Tor Britannia* (15,657/1975) and her sister ship, they could have been operated on a fortnightly service between the Liverpool terminal in Canada Dock and a pontoon alongside the passenger berth at Apapa, Lagos for, between 1971 and 1978 one of the company's four car carriers, *Clearway* (1,160/1970) had done just that between Poole and Apapa Quays every 28 days. A portent had been ignored and an episode of history had ended.

Photographed at Singapore, *Coral Princess* was briefly considered as a replacement for *Aureol*. [Russell Priest]

Carway, photographed on 20th August 1971, was one of four ro-ros operated by Elder Dempster. [J. and M. Clarkson]

Top: *Accra* deeply laden: her green boot topping is only just visible. *[Michael J. Ingham]*

Middle: *Apapa* at Liverpool with a lighter alongside: note the cargo cloths. *[J.K. Byass]*

Bottom: Anchored off Singapore on 15th March 1974, *Taipooshan* – the former *Apapa* – flies the house flag of Shun Cheong Steam Navigation Co. Ltd. at her main, plus the red ensign at her stern (she was registered in Liverpool) and a Singapore courtesy flag at her foremast. She looks in remarkably good external condition for a ship that would be sent to the breakers within a year. *[V.H. Young]*

Top: *Apapa* and *Aureol* provide a contrast in hull colours, with the former having been given red boot topping, possibly in connection with her sale to Shun Cheong. Note the staging beneath her name on the bow which suggests she is about to be renamed. *[J.K. Byass]*

Middle: a fine view of *Aureol*, flying Elder Dempster's swallowtail house flag and a Royal Mail pennant from her main mast. *[Russell Priest]*

Bottom: *Aureol*, still registered at Liverpool following her sale, arriving at a Spanish port on 15th August 1974. *[Russell Priest]*

107

SPLENDID SMALL SHIPS OF THE FAR EAST

Nigel Jones

The replacement of conventional cargo ships by cellular containerships for transporting break-bulk goods by sea rapidly gained momentum during the 1970s. Nonetheless, there were some regions of the world, notably China and the rest of South East Asia which, without the proper infrastructure needed to handle high volumes of containers, lagged well behind in this revolution. Inevitably containerisation eventually spread throughout the Far East, forcing a diminishing role for traditional cargo ships. Singapore, located off the southern tip of Malaysia, in particular attracted ships of this type for bunkering, loading or discharging cargoes using barges and other requirements. Hiring a launch at Singapore for viewing or photographing shipping at close quarters in the local anchorages was a straightforward matter until the introduction of the International Ship and Port Facility Security Code 2002. This article reviews a fascinating selection of the last generation of classic small cargo ships which traded in the Far East. All pictures were taken at Singapore unless otherwise stated.

Between 1946 and 1959 the yards of A. Stephen and Sons Ltd., Linthouse and Henry Robb Ltd., Leith constructed an impressive total of 34 handsome motor cargo ships for the Union Steam Ship Company of New Zealand Ltd. (USSCNZ), a member of the P&O Group. They were specially designed for service in the Australia, New Zealand and Pacific Islands trades with distinctive tall upright masts and relatively long derricks. Stephen's share of the building programme was 15 ships which averaged a shade below 3,700 gross tons whereas, with the exception of *Waimate* (3,506/1951), those built by Robb were smaller, ranging between 942 and 2,584 gross tons. During the 1960s USSCNZ introduced new ships fitted with deck cranes as well as ro-ro vessels. Consequently the writing was on the wall for the company's fleet of conventional vessels, compounded by the gathering momentum of the container revolution. Hence over the duration of a decade commencing in the mid-1960s these ships were gradually sold to other owners for further service in new spheres. It is worthy of note that, due to a total reorganisation of the P&O group in 1971, USSCNZ, along with its ship owning subsidiaries, was sold to Tasman Union Ltd. - jointly owned by New Zealand Maritime Holdings Ltd. and TNT Shipping (New Zealand) Ltd.

Built by Henry Robb Ltd.
The Malaysian-owned *Luna Marina* (942/1946), formerly *Kanna*, was basically a Second World War B type but differed in having an oil engine instead of steam reciprocating machinery. In 1981 she was sold to another Malaysian owner and renamed *Seng Giap*. On 30th December 1983 the ship grounded at Tanjong Datu, Sarawak, became flooded and was abandoned. Declared a constructive total loss, almost a year later she was refloated for breaking up locally. Photographed in the Eastern Anchorage on 16th June 1980.

Several of the Robb-built ships were purchased by King Line (Private) Ltd., which operated as part of the Golden Line (Guan Guan Shipping (Private) Ltd.) group of Singapore, and included a trio all purchased in 1971. The former name of *King Star* (1,946/1957) (top) is confirmed as *Koonya* by its remnants discernible nearly a decade after it was last officially displayed. Her funnel, partially obscured by the bridge and superstructure, is painted in her owner's customary colours of yellow with black top. She was demolished at Singapore and work commenced in February 1985. Photographed in the Eastern Anchorage on 12th February 1983.

Perhaps for operational reasons the *King Tower* (2,007/1957) and *King Horse* (1,952/1955), previously *Konini* and *Navua* respectively, wear Guan Guan's distinctive blue livery. The *King Tower* (middle) was scrapped at Jurong, Singapore, during 1985. Photographed in the Eastern Anchorage on 27th June 1980.

In this archetypal period scene, the *King Horse* (bottom) is discharging her cargo into local bum boats. She was well equipped for this type of work, which would have been a routine procedure in the Pacific Islands trades for which she had been designed. In 1985 she became the Honduran-registered *Kin Horse 1* and was deleted by 'Lloyd's Register' in the early-1990s. Photographed in the Eastern Anchorage on 27th June 1980.

The Malaysian-flag *Meladju* (2,007/1956) (top), ex *Kaimai* 1972, was a sister ship of *King Tower*. She subsequently carried the names *Kita*, *Sanua* and *Paisa*. She was broken up in Thailand during 1987. Photographed in the Eastern Anchorage on 28th June 1980.

The *Kaitoa* (2,584/1956) was sold in the early-1970s and subsequently owned at various times by Panamanian or Malaysian companies. Throughout most of the 1970s she traded as *Katoa* but was renamed *Hati Baik* in 1979 (middle). At the very respectable age of 36 *Hati Baik* arrived at Singapore in July 1992 for breaking up. Photographed in the Eastern Anchorage on 18th June 1980.

The general cargo ship lines of Indonesian-owned *Gembira* (2,385/1948) (bottom)are deceptive and provide few, if any, clues that she was designed primarily for the New Zealand coal trades. Completed as *Kaitangata*, she was notable for being the first in a series of six similar USSCNZ colliers (although *Kokiri* (2,470/1951) had minimal cargo gear) all of which were delivered by Robb between 1948 and 1951. The *Gembira*, her fourth name after disposal in 1968, suffered extensive damage due to an engine room fire breaking out on 6th March 1981while lying off Teluk Bayur, Indonesia. Declared a constructive total loss, five months later she was delivered to Indonesian breakers at Cigading. Photographed in the Eastern Anchorage on 20th June 1980.

Built by A. Stephen and Sons Ltd.
The mid-1970s heralded a substantial reduction in the number of ships owned by USSCNZ which involved the elimination of its remaining conventional vessels. A case in point is the *Koranui* (3,722/1956). She was purchased by Maldives Shipping Ltd. in 1975 and renamed *South Pacific*. In 1977 she was transferred to a Panama-registered company and two years later renamed *Pride of Baghdad*. In 1984 the ship was acquired by other Panamanian owners and renamed *Kutub Star*, but later the same year she was sold to Bangladeshi breakers at Chittagong. Photographed in the Western Anchorage on 18th June 1980.

Built in Scotland for other owners
The *Sang Fajar* (3,155/1947), owned by the Malaysian International Shipping Corporation Berhad, was built by A. and J. Inglis Ltd., Glasgow as *Soochow* for the China Navigation Co. Ltd. She was one of a quartet of similar S class ships designed for the company's South China and Thailand emigrant trades. However, after the Second World War this trade diminished to the point that only one vessel was required. Consequently, *Soochow* was used initially for Hong Kong, Philippines and Australia voyages and later mainly Australia to Papua New Guinea services. In 1967 she was acquired by newly-formed Pacific International Lines (Private) Ltd. (PIL), Singapore and became *Kota Ratu*. She continued trading for PIL until transferred to the Malaysian company in 1975. *Sang Fajar* was sold for breaking up at Kaohsiung in 1984. It is worthy of note that she survived her three sister ships by a considerable margin; they were all broken up during 1978. Photographed in the Western Anchorage on 15th June 1983.

Maldives Shipping Ltd., incorporated in 1967, expanded at a phenomenal rate during the 1970s by purchasing, from various owners good quality tonnage mainly constructed at Northern European or Scandinavian yards. The company's vessels were frequently noted at Singapore such as ex-British pair *Maldive Trader* (3,218/1959) (above) and *Maldive Pearl* (2,769/1956) (below).

Maldive Trader was built by Hall, Russell and Co. Ltd., Aberdeen and delivered to the Donaldson Line Ltd. as *Santona*. At Glasgow in 1966 Barclay Curle lengthened the ship

as well as fitting a second mast and supplementary derricks. A year later Donaldson disposed of its shipping interests to G. Heyn and Sons Ltd. of Belfast. *Santona* was retained until 1974 and then sold to Maldives Shipping. On 9th January 1983 *Maldive Trader* stranded on the North Jumna Shoal, Sudan, but was refloated later the same day. A subsequent inspection at Karachi found that she was beyond economical repair. She arrived at Gadani Beach, Pakistan for demolition in April 1983. Photographed in the Eastern Anchorage 20th June 1980.

Maldive Pearl was completed by Henry Robb as the *Flaminian* for Ellerman Lines Ltd. Following a reorganisation of the Ellerman group in 1974 she became *City of Izmir* but a year later was sold to Climax Shipping Corporation, controlled by Maldives Shipping Ltd., and renamed *Climax Pearl*. In 1981 she was transferred to Maldives Shipping and, in keeping with the company's nomenclature practice, became *Maldive Pearl*. Ultimately she, too, arrived at Gadani Beach for breaking up, 12 months after the *Maldive Trader*. Photographed in the Western Anchorage on 12th February 1983.

The Thai-flag *Thani* (927/1949) was built as *Mamaku* by Henry Robb for the Anchor Shipping and Foundry Co. Ltd. of New Zealand., incorporated in 1901. She was specially designed to take into account length and draught requirements of certain New Zealand ports, such as Mapua, and operated in the general cargo or coal trades until laid up at Nelson in the early 1970s. In 1972 she was sold to Pacific Islands Transport Corporation of Vila, New Hebrides, and subsequently renamed *Mamatu*. In 1973 she was acquired by a Singapore owner and with a few strokes of a paint brush became *Mamani*. From the late-1970s her history is somewhat murky. Her identity as *Thani* was not officially recorded in the registers but by 1983 she was reported as the *Hai Soon Kao* of Bangkok. In March 1986 she was noted at Singapore as the *Hadyai Union 2*, another unofficial name. The ship was deleted from the registers in 1999. Photographed in the Eastern Anchorage on 28th June 1980.

Built by Goole Shipbuilding and Repairing Co. Ltd.

The *Ouolof* (1,586/1948) was built for Compagnie de Navigation Paquet of Marseilles, a firm well-established in the Mediterranean trades, particularly between French and North African ports. She had three cranes for handling cargo, which was sophisticated gear for a new ship of that era. In 1965 she was sold to Singapore-based Guan Guan affiliate King Line S.A. of Panama, joining its motley collection of elderly small vessels, and renamed *Apollo*. In 1976 she was transferred to Guan Guan Shipping Sdn. Berhad, Malaysia and became the *Golden Hill*. In 1978 she was acquired by Rosewell Maritime Co., Panama and renamed *Hai Hong*. In November the same year she arrived off Port Klang, Malaysia, carrying approximately 2,500 Vietnamese refugees, an event which drew widespread media coverage. For several weeks the Malaysian authorities would neither permit anyone ashore nor allow food provisions or other supplies to be loaded. Only after intervention by the international community did the refugees' desperate predicament come to an end. The *Hai Hong* was then laid up near Port Klang, where she sank on 5th May 1981. She was photographed on 24th June 1980.

Built in the Netherlands

The *King Bird* (1,326/1947) (above) was completed by Rotterdamsche Droogdok Maatschappij as *Batoela* for the Royal Netherlands Government and managed by Koninklijke Paketvaart Maatschappij (KPM). She was part of a class built by various Dutch yards to replace war losses in the Far East. The design dates from before the Second World War and was well suited for service in very hot climates. In 1952 ownership of *Batoela* was transferred to the managers. She was sold by KPM in 1960 to Metropole Lines, Panama and renamed *Bintang Mas*. Between 1964 and 1966 she

carried the names *San Miquel* (twice) and *Calabar*. She joined the fleet of King Line S.A., Panama in 1966 when she became the *King Bird*. Although subsequently the subject of occasional transfers between Guan Guan companies, she held this name until broken up at Jurong, Singapore, in 1983. Photographed in the Eastern Anchorage on 20th June 1980.

Between 1948 and 1950 a class of six *Si* ships was built by C. Van der Giessen and Zonen Scheepswerven, N.V., Krimpen a/d IJssel for KPM. *Sinabang* (2,193gt) had the distinction of being the first.

These ships operated on the company's various services involving ports of call in countries including Australia, Burma and India. In 1967 *Sinabang* was sold to Pacific International Lines (Private) Ltd .(PIL)and renamed *Kota Naga* (below). In January 1981 work began on scrapping her at Gadani Beach, Pakistan. It is worthy of note that in 1967/68 PIL also purchased *Si* class members *Siberoet*, *Sigli* and *Sibigo* which became *Kota Singa*, *Kota Eagle* and *Kota Machan* respectively. All three were scrapped in the early 1980s. Photographed in the Eastern Anchorage on 16th June 1980.

Built at Hong Kong

Pictured at Bangkok on 17th February 1983 the *Sri Thai* (612gt) (right) was, incredibly, still in service 70 years after she was built. Furthermore, she had a remarkably interesting career for a ship designed as a case-oiler. She was delivered by Taikoo Dockyard and Engineering Co. Ltd. to the Asiatic Petroleum Co. (North China), Shanghai as the twin-screw, diesel-engined *Ah Kwang* for service on the Yangtse Kiang River and Chinese coastal waters. By the late-1930s her owner had been renamed the Shell Co. of China. During the Second World War she was in service at Singapore between December 1940 and February 1942, followed by a very brief spell at Batavia before sailing for Colombo. Later war service included supplying the R.A.F. in North Africa with aviation fuel in drums. After the war, in November 1945, she sailed from Suez via Bombay to Shanghai and resumed her old trade and moved to Singapore in 1949. Her ownership details during the 1950s are sketchy though it is known that she did carry the names *Playaran* and *Rasmi*. In 1960 she was acquired by Madam Sutharom of Bangkok and renamed *Sri Thai*. The ship was deleted from 'Lloyd's Register' in 1960/61 but, surprisingly, was noted at Singapore in 1977. She was also observed at Bangkok in 1979 and Singapore, again, in 1981 which suggests that her twilight

years were spent trading between the two ports. Her fate is not known.

The diminutive *Sirivanich* (below) also has an exceptionally long and varied history. She was built by Hong Kong and Whampoa Dockyard in 1930 as the *Kurimarau* (288gt) for Lever's Pacific Plantations Propriety, Solomon Islands, a subsidiary of Lever Brothers Ltd., Port Sunlight. After the war she passed to the Solomon Islands Government, followed by the Pacific High Commission. In 1954 she operated for the Colony Wholesale Society, Tarawa Island, and in the same year was sold to S. Berg

and Co. Ltd. of Hong Kong. She was sold to Singapore owners in 1963 and three years later changed hands locally. Unusually, despite all these changes, she retained her original name. In 1966 she was deleted by 'Lloyd's Register' but a decade later amazingly turned up at Singapore. Therefore she must have passed to unspecified Thailand-flag owners, and renamed *Sirivanich* sometime between 1976 and June 1980. Significantly, she was last reported afloat near Krabi, Thailand, in 1995 but her continued existence must now be very doubtful. Photographed in the Eastern Anchorage on 22nd June 1980..

Built in Poland

In 1961 and 1962 Stocznia Szczecinska at Szczecin built for the Republic of Indonesia a class of seven B540 type cargo ships which were also capable of carrying up to 1,000 deck passengers and several more in cabins. A novel feature was a continuous shelter deck, giving full weather protection, which was intended for passenger use in traditional 'deck' style. At this level, too, large side ports were provided on both sides of the hull for ventilation purposes. The ships were each given a name beginning *To* and served in both the local and international services managed by The National Indonesian Shipping Company, established in 1952. The *Towuti* (3,357/1962), fifth ship of the series, is believed to have been broken up in Indonesia at the end of the 1980s. Photographed in the Eastern Anchorage on 13th February 1983.

Built by Norderwerft Koser & Meyer, Hamburg

The hull of Singapore-registered *Pacific Samudra* (1,902/1959) appeared to be in an exceptionally rusty and bio fouled state for a locally-owned vessel. She was built as *Clement* for the Booth Steamship Co. Ltd. of Liverpool, part of the Vestey Group. In 1964 the ship was returned to her builder for lengthening as well as installation of an additional mast and extra derricks. For nearly two decades *Clement* was

principally engaged in the trades from New York or Canadian ports to Manaus, North Brazil and the West Indies. After the service closed in 1977 she was laid up at Liverpool but sold the following year and renamed *Element* (Honduras flag). She traded as the *Pacific Samudra* between 1981 and 1984, owned by Greater Eastern Enterprises (Private) Ltd. She later carried the names *Gedong Emas* and *Indra Intan 2* for other owners. In 2010 IHS Fairplay reported her existence in doubt. Photographed in the Eastern Anchorage on 11th February 1983.

Built in Scandinavia

The *Gambela* was one of the last active split-superstructure cargo ships in the world. Moreover, she was an unusual scaled-down version of the type measuring only 1,603gt. She was constructed by Akt. Lindholmens Varv, Gothenburg, for Rederi A/B Svenska Lloyd and launched in 1943 but not commissioned as the *Industria* until July 1945; her hull was strengthened for navigation in ice. In 1962 she was purchased by Skibs A/S Karlander (Egil Paulsen), Norway, and renamed *Slinde*. Sold in 1965, she then traded as the Panamanian-registered *Paragon* until renamed *Hongkong Line* in 1974. She became the *Gambela* in 1975 following acquisition by a Singapore owner, though later was transferred to a Malaysian firm without changing name. She was deleted from 'Lloyd's Register' in the early 1990s. Photographed in the Eastern Anchorage on 11th February 1983.

A pair of ships from famous Danish yards, the *Hoe Aik* (2,923/1949) and *Hoe Hing* (1,705/1955), are pictured in the colours of Hoe Hoe Shipping Company of Singapore. Honduran-registered *Hoe Aik* was built by Burmeister & Wain, Copenhagen, and delivered to H/F Eimskipafelag Islands, Iceland, as *Lagarfoss*; the hull was strengthened for navigation in ice. A random selection of her voyage reports in the 1960s and 1970s suggest that she regularly visited Baltic and Icelandic ports and, sporadically, even U.S. ports. She was sold to a Singapore owner in 1977 and renamed *East Cape*, trading with this name until sold in 1980 when she became the *Hoe Aik*. She was deleted from the registers in 2002. Photographed in the Eastern Anchorage on 11th February 1983.

The Malaysian-owned *Hoe Hing* was constructed by Frederikshavn Vaerft and Flydedok A/S, Frederikshavn, as the *Naxos* for Det Forenede Dampskibs-Selskab A/S (D.F.D.S.) of Copenhagen. After a creditable 15 years' service she was sold and from 1970 to 1974 carried the names *Ulysses Ogygia*, *Calypso* and *Manuella Pride* for various Greek owners. In 1974 she was purchased by Hoe Hoe Shipping Company and renamed *Hoe Hing*. She was transferred to a Malaysian company in 1981, though she retained the same name. She arrived at Bangkok for breaking up in September 1983. Photographed in the Eastern Anchorage on 11th February 1983.

Record Books
IAN ALLAN 'ABC' BOOKS
Roy Fenton

Let's admit it: many of us were introduced to ships through the little Ian Allan 'abc' books. This editor was certainly 'converted' from train spotting by the availability of 'abc British Merchant Ships', kindling an interest still alive fifty years later. The abc books were on sale at pocket-money prices, and available widely through hobby shops and stationers as well as book shops (the last-named being something Ellesmere Port significantly lacked in the 1960s).

It is not entirely through the eye of nostalgia that these little pocket books retain such an attraction. Although imitated since (and the writer has both compiled and published such impersonations), the books remain a delight, because of all they pack in, the liberal use of excellent photographs and some fine cover designs. It helps, of course, that the ships illustrated were the last of the 'classic' ones that now feature strongly in 'Record'.

This article is an attempt to both chronicle and catalogue the abc range of merchant shipping books. It recognises that the books' offspring continue to be published by Ian Allan, although the 'abc' name has long been dropped (one wonders why). The imitators are not listed, and neither are Ian Allan's warship or yachting books. Nor is there any attempt to offer collectors a guide to price. Indeed, price is highly variable, as a significant number of the abc books surviving have been very well used, with ships underlined and in some cases additions and deletions to the ship lists made by hand.

The writer owes a considerable debt to M.G. Burbage-Atter who in 1991 compiled and published 'A Complete Guide to the ABC Pocket Books' which bravely set out to list the entire output of around one thousand titles. Burbage-Atter tentatively lists some possible editions but gives no information and, as the present writer has not been able to substantiate their existence, they have been omitted from the lists below. For instance, a possible 1961 edition of 'abc Foreign Coastal Freighters' is listed, but the author doubts the existence of a book he would undoubtedly have bought if he had seen a copy! Information on cover illustrations and authors has been added to the listings.

Forerunners
In 1942 Ian Allan began publishing his books for locospotters (he term he probably coined, but which never really stuck). He moved on to ships in 1946, aircraft in 1947 and buses in 1948. The early shipping books did not have 'abc' in their title, the first being 'Round the Southern Fleet' by Cuthbert Groseman. In 1947 'Ships of the Seven Seas: 1. The Passenger Liners' by Charles Graham appeared, but enthusiasts had to wait two years for its companion, 'Ships of the Seven Seas: 2. Merchant Ships'. These were 4½ by 6¾ inches and had 104 pages. The price increased from 3/9d for the first to 4/6d for number 2, even though quality deteriorated, with number 1 using art paper throughout and number 2 using it just for the photographs. The first volume had a short, general introduction giving a brief history of ships then rattling through parts of a ship, its crew, navigation,

watches and signalling. Eleven chapters dealt with each of the main British liner companies operating passenger ships, each getting a short history followed by descriptions of each of its ships, whether passenger or cargo. The introduction to the second volume was orientated more towards cargo ships, and also briefly covered ship building. Its 11 subsequent chapters covered a mix of British cargo liner and tramp owners dealt with in a similar way to volume 1. It then listed 16 other companies, and here could be seen the germ of the abc shipping books, in that each of these companies' ships simply had a one line entry, with name, machinery type, gross and deadweight tons and speed tabulated. The choice of which companies to include where seems to have been made at random: Clan, Blue Funnel and Federal Lines rub shoulders with Hogarth and Ropner in the more detailed section, with Ben, Blue Star, Furness Withy sharing the latter section with J. and C. Harrison and Reardon Smith. Although not quite as random, the distinction between liner and tramp companies continued to be somewhat blurred in compilers' minds, as the 'abc Ocean Freighters' editions listed Ben, Bank and Strick Lines amongst tramp operators.

The first abcs
The first of the 'true' abc shipping books was 'abc British Railways Steamers', with a print order dated June 1953. It had 48 pages, was 4 by 6 inches, making it uniform in size with the railway books, and cost 2/-. However, the format was untypical of later shipping books, with tabulations spread across two pages and including details such as fuel, accommodation and former owners which did not appear in other abc shipping books.

The format settled down with the first 'abc Ocean Liners' dated July 1953. This was also 4 by 6 inches, but was expanded to 64 pages, although some later abc books had a miserly 56 pages but still cost 2/6d. For each company a header gave company title, details of funnel and hull colours and a summary of routes, and for each ship were tabulated name, date, gross tonnage, length, breadth, speed, engine type and number of screws. With the omission of routes where inappropriate, and the addition of house flag details for Douglas Ridley Chesterton's editions, this format proved extremely durable. Throughout, photographic coverage was generous, and reproduction good although the page format was small. Early editions relied largely on 'official' photographs supplied by the shipping companies, but increasingly the work of excellent amateur ship photographers was used, including John G. Callis (many taken from the light vessel on which he worked), Ken Cunnington (famous for his Manchester Ship Canal portraits), Fred Hawks, George Osbon, Cliff Parsons, P. Ransome-Wallis and Roger Sherlock.

A major change came in 1965 when size was increased to 5 by 7¼ inches and 80 pages, and a number of editions were amalgamated. Sadly, the 1965 change in format was almost the swan song of the individual softbacks, which (apart from two later exceptions) disappeared after the 1966 editions.

'abc' was dropped from the titles in 1965, only for it to reappear in 1988 with W. Paul Clegg's 'abc British Shipping'. This book had an interesting concept, aiming to cover the ships of all major British companies, from tugs to VLCCs, now possible to fit in one 128-page softback because of the decline of British shipping. It even included potted histories of each company featured. But it ran to only one edition, probably because the hardback 'Ocean Ships' series was being published in parallel. Uniform in size and cover design was David L. Williams' 'abc Sea Traffic Management', also of 1988. Packing in a remarkable amount of information, this book was part of the publisher's estimable strategy of taking enthusiasts deeper into a subject. Again, it was not re-issued.

Burbag-Atter explains that an insight into print runs can be had through the print order codes which until 1963 appeared on the back covers; '750' being just that, but '100' indicating a thousand copies, and so on. The first 'abc Ocean Liners' of 1953 merited just 750 copies, but for all the 1954, 1955 and 1956 editions this was increased to 1,000 copies. The year 1957 saw growing interest, or at least confidence, with orders for most editions (surprisingly including the new 'abc British Trawlers') pushed to 1,250 and 'abc Ocean Liners' to 1,500. These figures held steady until 1959, when the order for 'abc Ocean Liners' was increased to 2,000 and the new 'abc Foreign Ocean Liners' to a confident 1,500. These probably represented the peak production runs, and it is noteworthy that the order for the second 'abc Foreign Coastal Freighters' in 1963 was reduced to 1,000 copies. A different series of print codes was used for subsequent issues.

Evolution of series

In the tables which follow the individual abc books are catalogued in the approximate order in which the first edition of a particular series appeared. Series tended to evolve, for instance 'abc Ocean Liners' became 'abc British Ocean Liners' when 'abc Foreign Ocean Liners' was published (the later incorporating and enlarging the small foreign section from 'abc Ocean Liners'). Often the edition numbers continued from the earlier to the later title (although the publisher was not consistent in including edition numbers, sometimes omitting them and in other cases just giving a date). In the case of these evolving editions, the separate titles have been grouped together.

The most complex example of evolution concerns the coastal shipping books. After 'abc Coastal Ships' of 1955, the title split into 'abc Coastal Cargo Ships' and 'abc Coastal Passenger Ships' (the latter also included some foreign ships). This series then spawned a completely new 'abc Foreign Coastal Freighters', the foreign liners remaining in 'abc Coastal Passenger Ships'. In 1966, in the general overhaul of the series, the four separate editions became 'British Coastal Ships' and 'Foreign Coastal Ships'.

'abc Ocean Liners' went through a similar evolution, listing some foreign liners until 1959 when it split into British and Foreign editions. However, 'abc Ocean Freighters' included no foreign ships, and the 'abc Foreign Ocean Freighters' was an entirely new book. In 1966, the titles became 'British Ocean Cargo Ships' and 'Foreign Ocean Cargo Ships'. Intermediate between the two were the tanker books, with 'abc Ocean Tankers' including a few purely foreign owners such as Texaco who migrated to 'abc Foreign Ocean Tankers', but the entire fleets of multinationals who had some British representation remained in 'abc British Ocean Tankers'.

The introduction of the books on foreign shipping presented the authors with a considerable challenge. Confining a title to British ships allowed a reasonably comprehensive coverage, although some small owners were omitted. But to stay within the bounds of the 64-page editions, authors had to be highly selective about which foreigners to include, especially when it came to coastal ships. H.M. Le Fleming and D. Ridley Chesterton both abandoned full listings when it came to the myriad Dutch coasters owned or more usually managed by the likes of Becks, Carebeka, Wagenborg and Wijne & Barends. Even so, this enthusiast was frustrated that the books did not help him identify many of the more interesting ships that visited the Mersey and the Humber in the 1960s. Perhaps this was a good thing, as it encouraged him to look at comprehensive sources of information such as 'Lloyd's Register'.

Cover illustrations

One of attractions of the abc books is the delightful scraper board illustrations on the cover of the early editions. There was more than one artist involved, but most were executed by A.N. Wolstenholme, who is credited on most of the illustrations. W.G. Eaton produced the dramatic, if slightly distorted, image of *Manchester City* on the cover of 'Ships of the Seven Seas: 2. Merchant Ships'. An illustrator named Haresnape took over for the 1959 editions, the last before photographs replaced illustrations.

Wolstenholme's *St. Patrick* first appeared on the cover of the pioneering 'abc British Railways Steamers' in 1953 and was also reproduced on the first edition of 'abc Coastal Ships' three years later, when it was credited to the illustrator. The only 'generic' illustration seems to be that on the first edition of 'abc British Trawlers', where Wolstenholme has drawn a fine motor trawler to which he gives the fictitious name 'Zarp'. Haresnape's Bank Liner on the 1959 'abc British Ocean Freighters' is one of the few illustrations which cannot be identified as a specific ship.

Black and white photographs made their appearance on covers with the 1960 editions. The format demanded a square photograph – not so common with the shape of the average ship. On the occasions where such an image was not available the cover is unsuccessful, as on the first edition of 'abc Foreign Ocean Tankers'. Initially, the identity of the ship on the cover was not revealed inside, and hence cannot always be named. An interesting anomaly is the cover of the 1960 'abc Coastal Cargo Ships' which has a photograph of a Fisher coaster with the name on the bow obliterated. It can be identified as *Lough Fisher* of 1950, which was wrecked in November 1959. It does not appear in the book's listings, but the choice of cover photograph must have already been made.

In a radical redesign, the 1965 editions saw the cover carry a combination of a line drawing and a photograph, accompanied with a price increase from 2/6d to 4/6d, but by 1966 it was back to photographs only.

Authors

Despite his promising start, Charles Graham who compiled the two 'Ships of the Seven Seas' was not involved in any of the 'true' abc books. No author is listed for 'abc British Railways Steamers' or its 1962 successor, which were probably compiled by office staff who would have a close working relationship with British Railways through the locomotive books. The first abc book author acknowledged, and the most prolific, was Hugh Murton Le Fleming. During his tenure, only one other author was involved; John S. Styring, an expert on flags and funnels, contributed the sole edition of 'abc Excursion Ships and Ferries'. From 1962, Douglas Ridley-Chesterton compiled a number of editions of the coastal ships, tugs and trawler books, whilst at this time Bert Moody took over the ocean ship books, acknowledging his debt to the late H.M. Le Fleming.

Cover designs

Although the shipping books remained recognisable as a series from 1953 to the virtual demise of the soft backs in 1966, the changes in details of the cover design were legion. Even the design of the abc logo was fluid, changing from circular in various forms, through triangular, briefly becoming square, square with rounded corners, pennant-shaped, then 'television screen' shaped, although continuing to incorporate Ian Allan's 'signature'. The cover design changed in parallel, as can be seen in the accompanying illustrations which aim to show each design variant of the softbacks, but not the colour variations between individual editions, which are listed in the tables below.

Why so many changes, as publishers are usually at pains to maintain the look of a series of books? It was perhaps loose control of design over a large publishing empire (Ian Allan produced over a thousand abc books, as well as many other titles), but it might also have been aimed at distinguishing different editions on the book stand, to encourage the punter to purchase the latest offering.

The softback abcs

In the list of the softback titles below, the date in the first column of each table is the print order date, which appeared as part of a code, usually on the back cover. This pre-dates actual publication, but – unless an edition is actually dated – is often the main clue to when the title appeared. In the few cases where this is not available, the date has been estimated from the completion year of the newest ships listed. The second column gives the number of the edition, the date printed on the title page, or the date given below the introduction (the editors were remarkably inconsistent here). The third column names the ship on the cover, the next the main colours used, then the author and in the final column the illustrator, or whether a photograph was used.

Despite much effort, the listings which follow may not be complete. The author would be delighted to hear of corrections or additions.

A further article is planned covering the combined volumes, the hard back successors to the abc books and other Ian Allan shipping books.

abc British Railways Steamers					
1953 June	-	*St Patrick*	Green/blue	Anonymous	Wolstenhome
British Railways Steamers and Other Vessels					
1962 May	-	*Cambria*	Blue	Anonymous	Photograph
abc Ocean Liners					
1953 July	-	*United States*	Blue/black	H.M. Le Fleming	Wolstenhome
1954 July	-	*Arcadia*	Yellow/blue	H.M. Le Fleming	Wolstenhome
1955 July	1955	*Saxonia*	Orange/blue	H.M. Le Fleming	Wolstenhome
1956 July	1956	*Empress of Britain*	Blue/yellow	H.M. Le Fleming	Wolstenhome
1957 October	5th	*Reina del Mar*	Blue/yellow	H.M. Le Fleming	Wolstenhome
1959 January	6th	*Rockhampton Star*	Orange/blue	H.M. Le Fleming	Haresnape
abc British Ocean Liners					
1959 November	7th	*Pendennis Castle*	Yellow/blue	H.M. Le Fleming	Photograph
1961 December	1962	*Empress of Britain*	Purple/yellow	H.M. Le Fleming	Photograph
1965 January	1965	*Canberra*	Yellow/blue	B. Moody	Photograph
1966 April	1966	*Carmania*	Blue/orange	B. Moody	Photograph
abc Foreign Ocean Liners					
1959 November	1st	*Fort Richepanse*	Orange/blue	H.M. Le Fleming	Photograph
1961 December	1962	*Statendam*	Blue/yellow	H.M. Le Fleming	Photograph
1966 January	1966	*Argentina or Brasil*	Orange/blue	B. Moody	Photograph
abc Ocean Freighters					
1954 August	-	*Wokingham*	Red/blue	H.M. Le Fleming	Wolstenhome
1955 July	1955	*Deerpool*	Red/green	H.M. Le Fleming	Wolstenhome
1956 July	1956	*Foylebank*	Green/yellow	H.M. Le Fleming	Wolstenhome
1957 November	4th	*Sussex Trader*	Red/blue	H.M. Le Fleming	Wolstenhome
abc British Ocean Freighters					
1959 January	5th	Bank Liner	Red/blue	H.M. Le Fleming	Haresnape
1961 November	1961	*Huntsmore*	Pink/yellow	H.M. Le Fleming	Photograph
1965 January	-	*Warkworth*	Purple/blue	B. Moody	Photograph

British Ocean Cargo Ships					
1966 April	1.1966	*Baluchistan*	Red/yellow	B. Moody	Photograph
abc Foreign Ocean Freighters					
1959 January	-	*Axeline Brodin*	Yellow/blue	H.M. Le Fleming	Haresnape
1961 November	1961	*Toronto*	Pink/yellow	H.M. Le Fleming	Photograph
Foreign Ocean Cargo Ships					
1966 April	1.1966	*Drakenstein*	Green/ochre	B. Moody	Photograph
abc Ocean Tankers					
1955 April	-	*London Splendour*	Brown/blue	H.M. Le Fleming	Wolstenhome
1956 April	1956	*British Corporal*	Brown/blue	H.M. Le Fleming	Wolstenhome
1957 August	-	*San Fernando*	Blue/orange	H.M. Le Fleming	Wolstenhome
1959 April	4th	*Vivien Louise*	Pink/blue	H.M. Le Fleming	Haresnape
abc British Ocean Tankers					
1960 July	5th	*Queda*	Pink/blue	H.M. Le Fleming	Photograph
1962 January	1962	*Athelfoam*	Green/yellow	H.M. Le Fleming	Photograph
1965	1.1965	*Oscilla*	Green/blue	B. Moody	Photograph
April 1966	4.1966	*Teesfield*	Purple/green	B. Moody	Photograph
abc Foreign Ocean Tankers					
1960 April	1st	Reksten tanker	Orange/blue	H.M. Le Fleming	Photograph
1962 January	1962	Ditlev-Simonsen tanker	Green/yellow	H.M. Le Fleming	Photograph
1966 April	1966	*Havbor*	Orange/purple	B. Moody	Photograph
abc Coastal Ships					
1955	-	*St Patrick*	Maroon/green	H.M. Le Fleming	Wolstenhome
abc Coastal Cargo Ships					
1956 July	1956	*Eleanor Brooke*	Brown/pink	H.M. Le Fleming	Wolstenhome
1958 April	3rd	*Sapphire*	Green/pink	H.M. Le Fleming	Haresnape
1960 March	4th	*Lough Fisher*	Orange/blue	H.M. Le Fleming	Photograph
1962 June	5th	*Celebrity*	Brown/green	D.R. Chesterton	Photograph
abc Coastal Passenger Ships					
-	1956	*Saint Columba*	Brown/green	H.M. Le Fleming	Wolstenhome
1958 April	-	*Duke of Lancaster*	Maroon/blue	H.M. Le Fleming	Wolstenhome
1960 January	4th	*King George V*	Turq./blue	H.M. Le Fleming	Photograph
1963 February	-	*Maid of Orleans*	Brown/blue	D.R. Chesterton	Photograph
abc Foreign Coastal and Short Sea Freighters					
1959 January	-	*Theano*	Green/blue	H.M. Le Fleming	Haresnape
1963 June	-	*Finkenau*	Brown/yellow	D.R. Chesterton	Photograph
British Coastal Ships					
1966 May	-	*Free Enterprise II*	Purple/orange	D.R. Chesterton	Photograph
Foreign Coastal Ships					
1966 May	-	*Kyholm*	Orange/maroon	D.R. Chesterton	Photograph
abc British Tugs					
1956 March	1956	*Marie Lamey*	Red/turquoise	H.M. Le Fleming	Wolstenhome
1957 September	2nd	*Formby*	Orange/green	H.M. Le Fleming	Wolstenhome
1960 March	3rd	*Plateau*	Buff/blue	H.M. Le Fleming	Photograph
1965 July	4th	*Maplegarth*	Orange/purple	D.R. Chesterton	Photograph
1966 May	5th	*Meeching*	Blue/green	D.R. Chesterton	Photograph
abc British Trawlers					
1958 January	-	Generic trawler	Brown/grey	H.M. Le Fleming	Wolstenhome
1963 June	-	*Ross Archer*	Green/brown	D.R. Chesterton	Photograph
abc Excursion Ships and Ferries					
1958 June	-	*The Mew*	Pink/green	John S. Strying	Wolstenhome

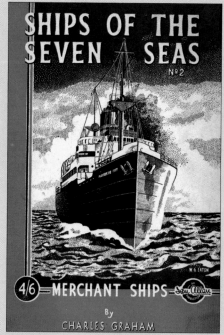

The two volumes of 'Ships of the Seven Seas', published in 1947 and 1949, and forerunners of the 'abc' books.

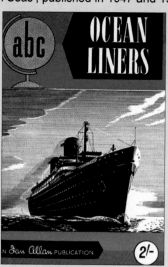

The first abc books, published in 1953. Note the different treatments of the abc logo, and Wolstenholme's dramatic depiction of the *United States*.

In 1954 'abc Ocean Freighters' joined 'abc Ocean Liners'; 'Ian Allan' was added to the logo.

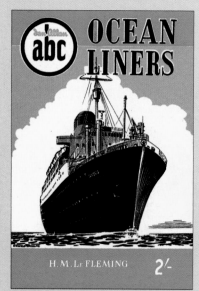

Uniquely, the 1954 format was re-used in 1955 for a series expanded with 'abc Ocean Tankers' and 'abc Coastal Ships'

A change of format for 1956 saw the range grow to seven books, with coastal ships split into two volumes.

The first edition of 'abc British Tugs' in 1956 saw the author's name treated in a different style from other 1956 editions.

The cover design of the 1957 'abc Ocean Tankers' appears to have been a one-off.

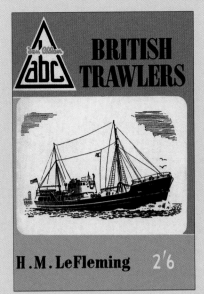

Additions in 1957/58 were 'abc British Trawlers' and 'abc Excursion Ships and Ferries'.

The two coastal books for 1958 had a change to the cover typography.

in 1959 came 'abc Foreign Coastal Freighters' and 'abc Foreign Ocean Freighters', new covers and a new illustrator.

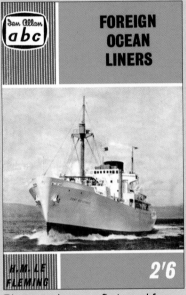

Photographs were first used for the 1960 editions, which included 'abc Foreign Ocean Liners' and 'abc Foreign Ocean Tankers'.

In 1962/63 the logo changed again and the brown 'pinstripe' was used on each cover of a reduced range of editions.

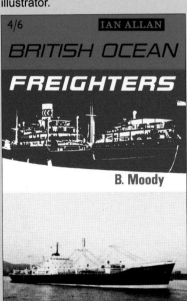

The post-modernist cover design of 1965 was thankfully a one-off.

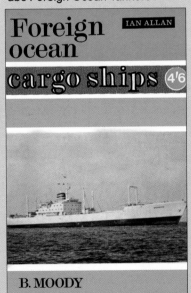

1966 saw a new larger size, revised titles, but no 'abc'.

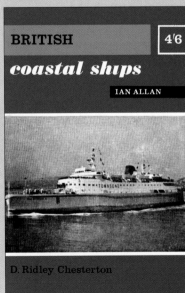

The 1966 coastal ships pair adopted yet another cover design.

FIFTY YEARS AT EASTHAM
Roy Fenton

With my family quite indifferent to ships, and none having had a career at sea, my own interest in shipping was stimulated largely by living within two miles of what was, in the 1950s and 1960s, one of the most perfect places to watch and photograph ships. At Eastham on the Mersey one got close to ships as they prepared to enter or sailed from the Manchester Ship Canal, those inward bound usually lingering whilst locks were prepared. For photographers, the sun was behind the camera for most of the day, whilst the width of the Mersey at that point meant little in the way of distracting background clutter. Over the years tens of thousands of shots have been taken at Eastham by excellent photographers. In the half century since I first took my camera there, I have managed to get a few colour images which I, at least, have been satisfied with or which have a story attached.

PLAINSMAN
William Doxford and Sons (Shipbuilders) Ltd., Sunderland, 1959; 8,732gt, 489 feet
2SCSA 6-cyl. oil engine by William Doxford and Sons (Engineers) Ltd., Sunderland
On Saturday 18th May 1969 I was late arriving at Eastham, and drove up in my Morris Minor just as Harrison's *Plainsman* was passing the ferry. I leapt out and grabbed this shot, with no time to frame it and limited by the only lens I possessed. A couple of months later I entered it for the slide competition at the Manchester Branch of the World Ship Society, and was astounded to win first prize – the first and only time my photography has been awarded anything.
    Plainsman was half way through her life with Harrison Line when photographed. She was sold in 1979 to the inevitable flag-of-convenience owner and as *Evlalia* served until 1982 when laid up near Piraeus. From there she was towed to Aliaga for demolition early in 1985.

MAIDAN
William Hamilton and Co. Ltd., Port Glasgow, 1946; 8,533gt, 504 feet
Two steam turbines double-reduction geared to a single shaft by David Rowan and Co. Ltd., Glasgow
I was fortunate enough to begin colour photography whilst there were still classic steam turbine-driven cargo liners in everyday service, and caught Brocklebank's *Maidan* gingerly approaching the Eastham Locks on 17th August 1969. One exposure per ship was all that was affordable, and – three months after photographing *Plainsman* – the same film was in my camera.
    Maidan was soon sold. As *Pretty* and later *Taighetos* she worked until 1972 when, after grounding damage, she was broken up in Taiwan.

MARIA N
Barclay, Curle and Co. Ltd., Glasgow,
1941; 5,291gt, 426 feet
Doxford-type 2SCSA 4-cyl. oil engine by
Barclay, Curle and Co. Ltd., Glasgow
It was still possible to photograph war-
built ships in 1970, and *Maria N* had
quite a history. She was built as *Empire*
Glade relatively early in the war, and did
not escape damage, being shelled by
U 67 in the North Atlantic in November

1942, although being able to complete
her voyage to Charleston for repairs.
Soon after the war her then managers,
G. Heyn and Sons Ltd., added her to the
fleet of their Ulster Steamship Co. Ltd. as
Innishowen Head. This she served until
1962, when a subsidiary of the London-
Greek Loucos Nomikos bought her and
renamed her *Maria N* under the Greek flag.

The stern view shows to good
effect her highly colourful Nomicos

funnel, and is also interesting in that no
tugs are assisting her, confirmed by a
previous bow view. Note the hobbler's
boat coming to take her lines. Her
good external state suggests she was
being looked after, and she survived
until 1972 when she was broken up
near Istanbul.
Despite the wintry-looking trees, the
date is 26th April 1970, spring arriving
decidedly late in Cheshire that year.

ESSI KARI
A/B Gotaverken, Goteborg, 1956; 10,696gt,
490 feet
7-cyl. 2SCSA oil engine by A/B Gotaverken,
Goteborg
Adding to the variety of ships seen in
the Ship Canal were chemical tankers
belonging to Norwegian owner Ruud-
Pedersen, carrying the extremely

unpleasant tetra-ethyl lead, an anti-knock
ingredient for petrol, from a plant near
Ellesmere Port. One of their number, *Essi*
Kari sails from Eastham on 7th April 1973,
Rea's tug *Hazelgarth* having the apparently
simply task of helping her out of the lock
and a few hundred yards down the river.
Although chemical tankers
are the commonest craft now seen at

Eastham, the Ruud-Pedersen ships
are long departed, as of course is the
addition of lead to petrol. *Essi Kari* was
the former ore carrier *Arjeploj*, converted
to a chemical tanker in 1965. Greenpeace
would not approve of her disposal:
contaminated with tetra-ethyl lead, on
21st April 1982 she was towed out of the
Mersey and scuttled in the North Atlantic.

TAGUS (above)
*Astilleros del Cadagua,
Bilbao, 1970; 1,578gt,
280 feet
6-cyl. 4SCSA oil engine
by N.V. Werkspoor,
Amsterdam.*
The shot of *Tagus*
sailing on Ellerman's
container service to
the Iberian Peninsula
on 6th November 1973
recalls Ellesmere Port's
modest career as a
container terminal. Its
success was partly due
to dock labour troubles
at Liverpool but, when
these were resolved,
the senior port had no
problem in undercutting
Ellesmere Port, and
even its rather basic
container crane was
soon removed.

    Tagus was chartered from Sea
Containers Ltd., one of eight 'Hustler'
class ships. When Ellerman decided
to adopt City names, she became *City
of Lisbon* in 1974. Off charter in 1979
she was renamed *Cape Hustler*, a name
subsequently shortened to *Cape*. As
Despo she foundered in the eastern
Mediterranean during November 1989
    The photograph of *Tagus*
was taken from the Eastham Locks
themselves: note the closeness to the
dolphins marking the beginning of the
channel. In those happy pre-ISPS days,
photographers wandering along the
Canal itself were tolerated, at least at

weekends. I remember being somewhat
concerned one day when a police car
drew up alongside me whilst I was taking
a shot. The panic subsided when I
realised its policeman driver had also
come to photograph a ship.

MANCHESTER CONCORDE (above)
*Smith's Dock and Co. Ltd.,
Middlesbrough; 1969; 12,040gt, 530 feet
Pielstick-type 18-cyl 4SCSA oil engines
by Crossley Premier Engines Ltd.,
Manchester*
Given the emptiness of the Canal now,
it is difficult to believe that forty years
ago it made history by hosting the first
British line to run a fully-containerised

oceanic service. *Manchester Concorde*
was Manchester Liners' third cellular
ship for their route to Montreal. Given
that they were of the maximum size for
the Canal's locks, it should have been
apparent that any growth in the size of
container ships would eventually rule out
Manchester as a terminal port, and so it
proved.
    The date is 10th February 1974,
and beyond *Manchester Concorde* can
be seen the now-demolished cooling
tower of Bromborough Power Station.
Sold in 1982 to Taiwan owners and
renamed *Char Lian* she lasted only until
December 1983 when she was broken
up at Kaohsiung.

STOLT VISTA (above)
Kockums M/V A/B, Malmo; 1955,
16,207gt, 596 feet
8-cyl. 2SCSA oil engine by Kockums M/V
A/B, Malmo
The ore carriers of Trafik A/B
Grängesberg-Oxelösund were once a
not unusual sight on the Manchester
Ship Canal, carrying Swedish iron
ore to the steel works at Irlam. It
was a pleasant surprise to be able
to photograph one of the company's
distinctive ore-oil carriers making

a return visit, albeit in a somewhat
different guise.
    Vistasvagge as she had been
built, was renamed *Stolt Vistasvagge* in
1970, and this was shortened to *Stolt
Vista* on her 1973 sale to her former
charterers, the chemical tanker operators
Stolt-Nielsens Rederi A/S of Haugesund
who put her under the Liberian flag.
There is no record in 'Lloyd's Register' of
her being converted to a chemical tanker,
so Stolt must have used her original holds
for their chemicals.

    I was doubly lucky in
photographing her on 11th May 1974 as
she was sold that year, going to Greek
owners as *Eleistria VII*, as which she was
demolished at Barcelona in 1979.

BRIDGEMAN (left)
Hall, Russell and Co. Ltd., Aberdeen,
1972; 3,701gt, 340 feet
16-cyl. 4SCSA oil engine by Ruston
Paxman Diesels Ltd., Colchester.
Even with a modest degree of
trespassing, getting a decent shot of
a tanker in the Queen
Elizabeth II Oil Dock usually
eluded the author. The best
that could be achieved, at
least legally, was from a road
above and to the south of
the dock when a tanker like
Rowbotham's *Bridgeman*
was on the western berth.
    The date is 1st
December 1974, the
Belgian-flag Gulf Oil tanker
alongside is *Belgulf Progress*
(12,018/1959), but I did not
record the identity of the
other tanker about to enter
the oil dock.
    In 1994 *Bridgeman*
was sold by P&O (who
had obtained control of
Rowbotham in 1993). She
subsequently sailed as
Sandy and is currently
Nejmat el Petrol XXV.

EUCADIA (above)
Hawthorn, Leslie (Shipbuilders) Ltd., Newcastle, 1961; 5,924gt, 468 feet Doxford-type 5-cyl. 2SCSA oil engine by Hawthorn, Leslie (Engineers) Ltd., Newcastle

Following its acquisition by Walter Runciman and Co. in 1965, Anchor Line ran to Manchester. As part of what was almost a reverse takeover, some Runciman ships were transferred to Anchor ownership, including the *Linkmoor* which became *Eucadia* in 1968. She is seen after a rainstorm on 23rd November 1974, with a backdrop of the Cheshire hills around Helsby and Frodsham, the towers of Stanlow Refinery and Mount Manisty alongside the Ship Canal. Alexandra tugs are in attendance, reminding me of the enthusiasm for Eastham of the late Jim Nelson, himself a tug skipper. Like him,

I can remember when it was possible to see there ship handling tugs from five different operators: Alexandra, Lamey, Liverpool Towage's Cock tugs, Rea, and the Manchester Ship Canal – although tugs of the last-named never routinely came out of the locks.

Eucadia was sold in 1981 and as the Sri Lankan-registered *Sigirya* was broken up at Gadani Beach in 1983.

CENTURY (opposite page, bottom)
Goole Shipbuilding and Repairing Co. Ltd., Goole; 1956; 770gt, 204 feet 'O'-type 6-cyl. 2SCSA oil engine by the Newbury Diesel Co. Ltd. Newbury.
This photograph was taken *near* Eastham, with the assistance of a Mersey ferry. On its way between Liverpool and Manchester one of the then irregular Co-op Travel cruises was approaching Eastham, fortuitously just before high water, so there were numerous ships about. Everard's *Century* had just sailed from Eastham Locks .

The date was 6th September 1975 and *Centurity* was another ship that was soon to be sold. Later that year she went under the Cypriot flag as *Tempesta*. Her fate is unknown: 'Lloyd's Register' deleted her for lack of information in 1987.

PARTINGTON (above)
Grangemouth Dockyard Co. Ltd., Grangemouth, 1965; 982gt, 201 feet 6-cyl 2SCSA oli engine by British Polar Engines Ltd., Glasgow
For many years, Eastham was associated with Shell vessels of various sizes. Tied up in canal just up from the locks on 7th November 1976 was their coastal tanker *Partington*, with the Lancashire side of the Mersey clearly experiencing a storm.

By the time the photograph was taken *Partington* carried the familiar Shell funnel, the joint marketing arrangement which saw ownership by Shell Mex and B.P. Ltd. having ended in 1975. She was briefly renamed *Shell Scientist* in 1979, but in 1981 crossed the Atlantic to Canada where she has carried the name *Metro Sun* and is currently *Hamilton Energy*.

INZHENER KREYLIS (left)
Hollming Oy, Rauma, 1975; 4,009, 124 metres Pielstick-type 16-cyl. 4SCSA oil engine by Oy Wartsila Ab, Turku/Abo
Approaching Eastham Locks from Ellesmere Port on 8th April 1977 is another ship which represents part of Ellesmere Port's changing fortunes as a port. The USSR's ro-ro *Inzhener Kreylis* ran on a service to the Baltic republics, but which was probably uneconomic for all but a subsidised state shipping line.

In 1991 transfer to Latvian ownership saw her name rendered *Inzenieris Kreilis*, as which she was broken up at Aliaga in 2002.

NORTHERN STAR (above)
Moss Rosenberg Verft A/S, Moss, 1980;
707gt, 65 metres
8-cyl. 4SCSA oil engine by A/S Bergens
M/V, Bergen

Do not put your camera away in winter. This photograph was taken on the Winter solstice, 21st December 1986, when the tide was just right for the short, sunlit hours.

Northern Star was a chlorine tanker, and because of the extreme toxicity of her cargo precautions to protect the crew included a gas-tight wheelhouse and accommodation. She was built to work between Warrington and Londonderry on behalf of the chemical company Dupont, replacing the Dutch *Marwit*, originally a dry cargo coaster equipped to carry chlorine in tanks installed below deck.

Northern Star retired from this onerous service in 2000, was converted to a products tanker and renamed *Norvarg*.

CITY OF MANCHESTER (below)
Appledore Shipbuilders Ltd., Appledore,
1979; 1,599gt, 316 feet
3-cyl. 2SCSA oil engine by Doxford
Engines Ltd., Sunderland

City of Manchester belonged to Cunard Ellerman Shipping Services Ltd., a merger of the interests of two old-established British companies running to the Mediterranean when both were acquired by Trafalgar House. The service was still running from Ellesmere Port when the photograph was taken on 8th May 1988, the container ship framed by trees and the old Eastham Ferry pier.

City of Manchester, which was built and engined in the United Kingdom, was named *City of Hartlepool* prior to 1985. Following sale in 2007 she has carried the names *City*, *Zeeland* and *Golden Bay*.

ETIENNE SCHLUMBERGER (above)
Chantiers Navales de la Ciotat, La Ciotat, France,1982; 6,165gt, 114 metres
Burmeister & Waine-type 6-cyl. 2SCSA oil engine by Alsthom-Atlantique, St Nazaire, France
Even if the light was not brilliant, the Mersey could sometimes be relied upon for dramatic cloudscapes. On 11th August 1988 the rather unattractively-named, Liberian-registered, Norwegian-managed, French-built liquid gas tanker *Etienne Schlumberger* approaches the locks, probably bound for one of the gas berths at Ince, adjacent to Shell's Stanlow Refinery.

Gas tankers tend to be long-lived ships, as their cargo is 'clean' compared with many petroleum derivatives, and maintenance standards have to be high. *Etienne Schlumberger* is still in service in 2011 as *Castorgas*, having already carried the names *Norgas Transporter*, *Eildon* (for George Gibson and Co. Ltd.) and *Sigas Eildon*.

KERNE (left)
Montrose Shipbuilding Company, Montrose, 1913; 63gt, 75 feet
T. 3-cyl. by W.V.V. Lidgerwood, Coatbridge, Glasgow.
Chronologically the last photograph in this sequence is of the oldest vessel I ever photographed at Eastham, the preserved steam tug *Kerne*. It was Sunday 16th May 2010, and she was returning to her Liverpool base making the last of a series of short cruises in connection with the World Ship Society's Annual General Meeting at Ellesmere Port. Quite possibly, the odd reader of 'Record' may recognize himself on board.

She was completed for the Admiralty as *Terrier* and used in Chatham Naval Dockyard until in 1948 she passed to J.P. Knight who gave her the name *Kerne*. This she retained after being acquired by Liverpool Lighterage Co. Ltd. and brought to the Mersey. Since retirement in 1971 she has been owned and operated by a group of enthusiasts, who have succeeded – where several museums have failed – in keeping a vintage coal-burner seaworthy and operational. *Kerne* reaches her centenary in two years time.

PUTTING THE RECORD STRAIGHT

Letters, additions, amendments and photographs relating to features in any issues of 'Record' are welcomed. Letters may be lightly edited. Note that comments on multi-part articles are consolidated and included in the issue of 'Record' following the final part. Senders of e-mails are asked to include their postal address.

Grand Union (Shipping) Ltd.

According to my files the *Blisworth* ('Record' 49, page 33) arrived for the first time in Antwerp after its re-opening to Allied shipping on Christmas Day 1944 from London. The vessel was then under command of Captain Bore and was the 373rd registered vessel to call after the re-opening of the port at the end of November 1944.
FLORENT VAN OTTERDYK, Antwerpsesteenweg 40, B-2070 Burcht, Belgium.

Clipper follow-up

The rescue of the crew of the *Bonita* ex-*Beringcore* ('Record' 47, page 159) took part in force 10-12 conditions after the ship had taken a sudden 45 degree list and the lifeboats could not be launched. The survivors were all rescued by attaching themselves to a line from the RNLI lifeboat and jumping one at a time from the stern of the ship. The rescue was well publicised and the coxswain was awarded a gold medal with all other crew members receiving a bronze medal.
TONY BREACH, Playas, Marcross, Vale of Glamorgan CF61 1ZG

Having read Tony Breach's article on the 'Clipper Boats' (Record 47 to 49) in particular the photo of the *Trojan Star* having sailed on her maiden voyage from Europe to the Gulf with frozen chickens and the charterer went bust, brought the memories flooding back and all bad.

Although you can not dispute the fact that most of them had long and useful life spans, they were badly

designed and were only made to work by the people who sailed on them. For instance, they had no 'fridge flat and the brine room was accessed by limboing under the prop-shaft.
A.D. FROST, 32 Oakfield Close, Sunderland SR3 3RT

Robertson follow-up follow-up

Regarding the Robertson history ('Record' 49), I was well aware that the photo on the title page is of the *Pearl* at Waterford. I have this photo in my collection and it shows her at the north (i.e. Kilkenny) side of the river at the coal yard of McCullagh. They traded as Wallace and McCullagh Ltd. with offices at 29 and 30 Quay, Waterford which would be directly across from their yard. They had a branch at Paul Quay, Wexford and they described themselves as 'Coal Importers, Ship Owners and Ship Chandlers. Shipwrights'. In the crowded notepaper headings of the day they also said 'Successors to Alexander Nelson'. By the time the photo was taken their notepaper had a less lot verbiage but had a lovely engraved vignette of coal hoppers, cranes, railway wagons and a steamer alongside and the title amended to 'McCullagh Ltd.'

Robertsons ships always seem to jump out at you in old picture postcards even in crowded dock scenes. Incidentally, I notice the famous white band early on in a couple of views seems to go right around the bridge structure; this is apart from one or two elongated incidences on some early motor ships.

However, to turn to the shot of *Pearl* I feel that Ian Wilson is muddying the waters in suggesting that 'it might have been taken by John Anderson who traded as Spindrift Photos'. I used to buy cards from him (the quality of the printing left an awful lot to be desired); but I seemed to understand that Anderson was an elderly, retired shellback. My real question is to ask if he was ever the photographer or merely earning a few bob in those bad old days by selling prints. The story I heard is that Jimmy Hartery loaned him a lot of negatives. Jimmy tried to get his negatives

Andy Skarstein kindly sent this slide of *Edinburgh Clipper* taken in Gothenburg on 22nd July 1975 and looking rather the worse for wear. Bob Todd points out that her tonnages were incorrectly recorded in 'Record' 48 and should be 3,632/2,636n 9,193/7,722d.

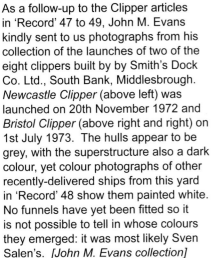

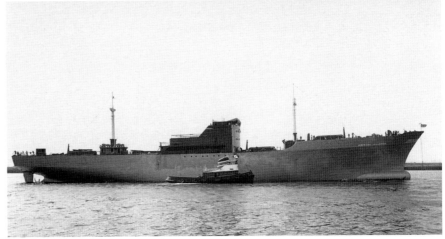

As a follow-up to the Clipper articles in 'Record' 47 to 49, John M. Evans kindly sent to us photographs from his collection of the launches of two of the eight clippers built by by Smith's Dock Co. Ltd., South Bank, Middlesbrough. *Newcastle Clipper* (above left) was launched on 20th November 1972 and *Bristol Clipper* (above right and right) on 1st July 1973. The hulls appear to be grey, with the superstructure also a dark colour, yet colour photographs of other recently-delivered ships from this yard in 'Record' 48 show them painted white. No funnels have yet been fitted so it is not possible to tell in whose colours they emerged: it was most likely Sven Salen's. *[John M. Evans collection]*

back when John Anderson died but it was too late and I am advised that they ended up in the World Ship Photo Library. Jimmy let it go (he was that sort of retiring type) happy, I think, that his main collection was safe in the hands of the late Dick Scott. As Jimmy gave me some albums with his original prints written up by himself I am satisfied as to the identity of the man behind the camera, many of which can be easily identified location wise. So the assumption that John Anderson was the photographer is, I think, unsafe.

Finally to go back to a wonderful issue 'Record' 2, I was fascinated by the view of the *Eurus* on page 127. I knew her from photos as *Kerry Head* so was intrigued by her four masts. You drew attention to her 'formidable array of masts and note too the supports for these on the port side'. Now this is the interesting bit. Goole ships carried derricks high up the mast to speed discharge in addition to those landed on crutches. Now I am fairly convinced that what we have on *Eurus* is some sort of sophisticated development of this. Note that the 'supports' are moveable.

Would you have access to contemporary shipbuilding journals which might throw some light on this and would anybody on the North East Coast know when they were removed?
TERRY O'CONALLAIN, 3 The Park, Skerries Rock, County Dublin.

The delightful photograph on page 126 may well be unique in showing the steam coaster *Calchfaen* (421/1893) under her original name, which she retained until 1916. She was built by the Ailsa Shipbuilding Company, Troon for Kneeshaw, Lupton and Company of Liverpool, owners who, as recorded in 'Mersey Rovers', operated a number of quarries in North Wales. Indeed, this is the only photograph known of a ship in Kneeshaw, Lupton colours, and strongly suggests that their funnel colours were yellow with a black top.

Because of the owners' trade, it is tempting to assume that the enormous chunks being laboriously loaded on to a selection of carts and wagons at St Peter Port, Guernsey are stone, but their slight sheen gives the game away: they are large pieces of coal from South Wales, no doubt destined for the island's greenhouses. Note the wooden ladder-like structures erected above *Calchfaen's* hatches, which allow the gangways to be kept fairly level during discharge: the tidal range at Guernsey is up to 28 feet. The photograph is dated around 11th September 1902, the *Calchfaen's* voyage having begun on 8th September.

Calchfaen has varnished masts and derricks, except for the mizzen mast which has a black upper part separated from the lower varnished part by a white ring. The steel work is painted and grained to simulate wood panelling. The lighter panels on the engine casing suggest that work on repainting these has paused whilst the coal is unloaded. A sail is rigged on the mainmast.

On sale in 1916, the Ailsa-built *Calchfaen* became *Glenshesk* of the Antrim Iron Ore Co. Ltd., Belfast. From 1927 to 1937 she was with a Francis Tyrrell, who operated out of Cardiff, and who latterly renamed her *River Avoca* reflecting his family's origins in the Irish port of Arklow. The ship left British registration in 1937 when sold to Albert Toop, Tallinn, Estonia who renamed her *Anna*. In October 1940 she was taken over by the British Ministry of Shipping, later the Ministry of War Transport, and became *Anna II*.

The captain/owner was, presumably, with her throughout the war, as in 1950 he registered her at Cardiff in the ownership of Albert W. Toop and Co. Ltd. as *Anna Toop*. She became familiar in the British coasting trade, perhaps because she was one of the few vessels to retain an open bridge. Apart from a slightly cut-down mizzen mast, the steamer was in remarkably original condition.

On 21st January 1958 *Anna Toop* stranded on Arklow Bank whilst on a voyage from Port Talbot to Londonderry with a cargo of steel plates. Although refloated, she sank the next day.

Thanks to Dr Charles Waine for his assistance with this caption. *[National Museum of Wales P2005.326]*

BOSUN'S LOCKER

You, our readers, never cease to surprise us with your depth of knowledge. We must admit that the pictures in 'Record' 49 were not of the best quality but you still managed to come up with some solutions for us. You sorted out the liner, also her accompanying tug, *Flying Falcon*, and the wreck - the *Porthcawl*. Whilst on the subject of *Porthcawl* I would have liked to include a picture of her before the fire, and having nothing of her, went on the Internet. A search for Porthcawl brought up many pictures of the town but a surprise was was on the

British Pathe News website which has a short sequence of her at sea on fire and after she had gone aground. Interesting if you have Internet access.

Photo 49/01
Both John Anderson and Geoff Holmes identify the ship as White Star's *Oceanic* built by Harland and Wolff in 1899. She transferred from Liverpool to Southampton in 1907. *Oceanic* was wrecked in the Shetlands in September 1914 whilst serving as an armed merchant cruiser.

ny Smythe identifies the paddle tug in this photograph
s *Flying Falcon*, based on photographs which appeared on
page 83 in 'Marine News' for February 1994 and on page
77 in 'The Clyde Shipping Company' by W.J. Harvey and
P.J. Telford. She was built in 1878 by J.T. Eltringham at
South Shields for Cork owners as *Lord Bandon*, passing
to Clyde Shipping and being renamed in 1886. In 1891
Flying Falcon was bought by Thomas Coggins of Liverpool
who kept her until 1902 when she was sold to France and
her hull used as a barge. Photograph 49/02 was almost
certainly taken on the Mersey between 1891 and 1902.

Tony has also worked on the identity of the
large steamer in 49/02, and reckons it is either *Servia* or
Aurania, built for the Cunard Steamship Co. Ltd. in 1881
and 1882 by J. and G. Thomson. *Servia* had a noticeably
shorter poop, and although the angle of the photograph
makes it difficult to be certain, Tony believes that it
shows this ship. *Servia* was broken up in 1902, the final
demolition work being carried out at Preston.

Photo 49/03

Alan Mallett identifies the wrecked steamer as *Porthcawl*
(2,481/1923) from an account in 'Wrecks and Rescues
off the East Anglian Coast', by the late Clifford Temple,
a noted Norwich historian, and published by Tyndale and
Panda Publishing in 1986 (ISBN 1870094 01 8).

On 14th September 1933, when the *Porthcawl*
was approaching the Happisburgh Light Ship, north of
Cromer, whilst on a voyage from Oran to Granton with
a cargo of 2,000 tons esparto grass, her Chief Officer
observed smoke coming from the port bunker. Attempts
to control or contain the fire by pumping water through
a hatchway failed, and the fire soon spread to the baled
esparto grass. At this point the ship was turned round
and made full speed towards Great Yarmouth with the
intention of beaching her. Unfortunately the fire quickly
spread, and the crew were taken off by the Gorleston
lifeboat, which had come in response to distress calls.
Meanwhile the fire proved an attraction to the late season
holiday makers, who crowded the front as the ship,
blazing spectacularly, drifted to and fro, at one point
threatening Britannia Pier. Local fishermen organised
boat trips round the wreck, albeit at a safe distance on
account of the extreme heat of the blaze. After a week,
the fire burnt itself out and the ship was nudged ashore
just south of the Britannia Pier.

The picture was probably taken soon after she
was grounded. Temple's book contains a later view with
both masts gone and the wreck within a few yards of the
shore. She was duly patched up and refloated on 26th
September and taken to Hull, where examination proved
her uneconomical to repair. She arrived at Sunderland on
17th December 1933 to be broken up by T. Young.

The white line above the anchors is the clue
which prompted Alan to dig out this useful but long-
unread book.

Porthcawl had been built in 1923 by the
Burntisland Shipbuilding Co. Ltd. for the Porthcawl Steam
Ship Co. Ltd. of Cardiff, managed by Thomas, Stephens
and Wilson Ltd. In 1932 she was sold, or probably merely
transferred, to Wilson and Harrison Steamships Ltd.
(Wilson and Harrison Ltd., managers), Cardiff.

Now for something different

We have received the following letter and a number of scans
from Guillermo C. Berger, a subscriber in Buenos Aires
and I quote: *I have now a riddle for you which you might
hopefully be able to solve, concerning identification of a
number of ship models in Rosario.*

*The original inquiry was submitted to the Histarmar
research group by officials of the Rosario branch of the
Liga Naval Argentina, an association supported by related
maritime industries but with strong support of the Argentine
Navy. Some years ago they had received two models from a
local maritime agency that closed down. They in turn have
passed these to the Museum of the Rosario Board of Trade,
where they are currently on display.*

One of the them is clearly the 1929-built Eastern
Prince *of Prince Line Ltd., a magnificent large model in a
reasonably good state of conservation. However, someone
presumably post-1982 and in a burst of nationalism, had
altered the name to* Rio Bermejo *on the bows, and as to
ascertain ownership put LIGA NAVAL ARGENTINA and
FILIAL ROSARIO as homeport on her stern. We hope that
for the sake of history this has now been rectified. This model
was however clearly identifiable as her case contained all
the relevant information on the plate at the base.*

*The other vessel is far more puzzling. It was in
a very bad state, and needed a 14-month restoration by a
professional modelmaker who had to manufacture missing
lifeboats, anchors and the propeller. It bore no name, but
several of the parts removed during the restoration process
had English inscriptions, so our first bet would be a British
ship. Moreover since during the first decades of the 20th
century the port of Rosario was the world's number 2 grain
trading hub, surpassed only by Chicago. And this trade was
mainly carried out by British tramp ships.*

*I have checked all my reference works for a match
of the ship and could not find any. I have both surveyed as
far as I could tramping concerns, and liner companies that
traded regularly to the river Plate. I would say that the vessel
should belong to the latter group because of her rather large
size, and for the number of portholes which would suggest
a vessel also engaged in the emigrant trades. But it is also
possible that these might be a later addition, as the number of
lifeboats seem not to correspond with a passenger carrying
vessel. There are also no access points to the below-deck
accommodation, other than the unusual side doors on the hull
(these again could point to a reefer ship). I would estimate her
building date between 1900-1920, again with a considerable
size for that era, and another unusual feature is the flush deck.
Any suggestions as to the identity of the ship will be welcome.*

*As described above and because of Rosario's
important position in the grain trades, many overseas
shipping companies had, if not indirect agency
representation, their own branch offices at the port. Among
them British concerns featured prominently, and they
frequently employed large models in frontline windows as
marketing tools. Many of these agencies have closed down
in the last decades, and where those models have ended up is
open to anyone's guess. We know of at least another agency
whose building was demolished some years ago and whose
models' collection has unfortunately gone astray.*

Thank you all for taking the trouble to study the
pictures. As we said at the start we are always amazed by the
informatipn you send to us.

Above: *Eastern Prince*, alias *Rio Bermejo*. The plate (above right) in the bottom left hand corner of the case confirms her identity but why name her *Rio Bermejo*?

Right: The mystery ship model. In a further view of the model the name *Liga Naval Argentina* has been painted on the bow. So, has anyone any idea of the original identity of this model or is it just a model of a typical ship? Our readers with a knowledge of ship models may be able to tell us more about the model even if it can't be named.

SOURCES AND ACKNOWLEDGEMENTS

We thank all who gave permission for their photographs to be used, and for help in finding photographs we are particularly grateful to Tony Smith, Jim McFaul and David Whiteside of the World Ship Photo Library; to Ian Farquhar, F.W. Hawks, Peter Newall, William Schell; and to David Hodge and Bob Todd of the National Maritime Museum, and other museums and institutions listed.

Research sources have included the *Registers* of William Schell and Tony Starke, 'Lloyd's Register', 'Lloyd's Confidential Index', 'Lloyd's Shipping Index', 'Lloyd's War Losses', 'Mercantile Navy Lists', 'Marine News', 'Sea Breezes' and 'Shipbuilding and Shipping Record'. Use of the facilities of the World Ship Society, the Guildhall Library, the National Archives and Lloyd's Register of Shipping and the help of Dr Malcolm Cooper are gratefully acknowledged. Particular thanks also to Heather Fenton for editorial and indexing work, and to Marion Clarkson for accountancy services.

Photographers at war
The second edition of 'Empire Ships' by Mitchell and Sawyer, published by Lloyds of London Press, provided much of the data concerning the British Government's wartime standard cargo ship programme, and historical information on the life of the Bartram ships featured. World Ship Society publications also consulted were 'Scrap and Build' by D.C.E Burrell, 'B.I', their history of The British India Steam Navigation Company by W.A. Laxon and F.W. Perry, and 'Convoys to Russia 1941-1945' by Bob Ruegg and Arnold Hague. The photographs were taken by W.L. Parry and Sons Ltd. and Frank and Sons of South Shields for Bartram and Sons Ltd, and given to the author. Information and photographs on the Isherwood 'Arcform' design can be found in 'Record' 1 and 9.

Splendid small ships of the Far East
Thanks to: Paul Boot, Roger Haworth (Miramar), David Hazell, Captain Michael Pryce, Graham Thursby, New Zealand Coastal Shipping (internet site of David Shepherd), New Zealand Ship and Marine Society, Lloyd's Register and Shipping of Goole (internet site). Publications consulted include K. O'Donoghue and S. Rabson 'P and O: A Fleet History' (World Ship Society, Kendal, 1988), Ian Farquhar 'Union Fleet' (New Zealand Ship and Marine Society Inc., Wellington, 2001) plus various editions of 'Marine News' and 'Sea Breezes'.

abc Books
M.G. Burbage-Atter 'A Complete Guide to the ABC Pocket Books' (Burbage-Atter, 1991) and the internet sites of various book dealers were consulted. Thanks also to Roger Sherlock and David Whiteside for their help, and to Mr Burbage-Atter for his personal help.

Robert Cock, Appledore Shipbuilder
'Record' 1 looked at Taw Shipyards Ltd., Barnstaple and 'Record' 14 and 15 at Hansen Shipbuilding, Bideford. Sources for the present article include Grahame Farr 'Shipbuilding in North Devon', Maritime Monographs and Reports No. 22, (National Maritime Museum, London, 1976); and Len Harris 'A Two Hundred Year History of Appledore Shipyards' (Hargill Partners, 1992) (the author Len Harris is the grandson of Philip K. Harris).

My Preston Ships and I
Unless otherwise credited, all photographs were taken by John Clarkson. David Whiteside is thanked for allowing access to his comprehensive records of Preston shipping movements.

Fifty years at Eastham
All photographs by the author.